Collecting Stamps

Other books by Paul Villiard

Collecting Stamps

Paul Villiard

With 77 photographs by the author

DOUBLEDAY & COMPANY, INC.
GARDEN CITY, NEW YORK
1974

ISBN: 0-385-01774-x Trade
     0-385-08677-6 Prebound
Library of Congress Catalog Card Number 73–10950
Copyright © 1974 by Paul Villiard
Printed in the United States of America
First Edition

TO GEORGE, KEN, AND TOM
My three philatelic friends
(Alphabetically catalogued)

Preface

———

Stamp collecting is a rich man's hobby. By rich, I mean *very* rich—like a multimillionaire? But hold on a minute. Stamp collecting is also a poor youngster's hobby. And it is an average person's hobby.

How can I say all these contradicting things about the same occupation? Its easy. A millionaire can go out, spend a quarter-of-a-million dollars, and come home with only *one* stamp! Yet a poor boy can go out—maybe even to the same stamp dealer, spend a quarter and come home with over a *hundred* stamps. And the average person can go to his post office, spend a few dollars and buy whole sheets of new stamps as they are issued, saving them until they rise in value, or, perhaps buying only the plate-number blocks, if that is his preference, paying only face value for them at the time. This is the beauty of stamp collecting. It is only as expensive as you want it to be, and it is within reach of every man, woman, or child in the world. That is what has put stamp collecting at the top of the list of hobbies, right along with tropical fish and rocks and minerals, which are the close second and third in order of popularity.

There are many reasons why people collect stamps. One of the main reasons is for investment. The people who buy stamps in the hope of making large profits are not really stamp collectors. They are not true *philatelists* because they have no real interest in the stamps themselves, but just think of them as articles that they buy cheap and sell for higher prices. Not that this is wrong. It is an excellent way to build up a nice bank balance if you know what you are doing. Usually, such an investor was for many years a real stamp collector, learning all about the little paper squares before he ventured into the investment market.

Then there are collectors who collect only those stamps that have to do with a given subject. This is called topical collecting, and topicals are a very big part of stamp collecting today. Perhaps a sports fan will collect stamps from all over the world having to do with baseball. His aim, as is the aim of every stamp collector of worth, is to obtain, in good condition, every single stamp ever published by every country in the world, with something about baseball as the motif. Any subject under the sun can be the subject of a topical collection. Next we have collectors who specialize in a particular country and are not interested in the stamps of the rest of the world. Some collect only new and unused stamps. Others wouldn't think of having any stamp in their collection that had not seen postal service.

No matter what your preference or the condition of your bank account, there is one area in stamp collecting that will interest you and that you can afford.

And not only this—stamp collecting is a valuable educational hobby. The person who collects stamps of a particular country, learns about its geography, history, art, music, industry, farming, politics— about nearly everything connected with that country.

The philatelist follows the changing map of the world in his little pieces of gummed paper. Countries that are no longer in existence have left their stamps behind them. Countries that come into existence during the lifetime of the young collector— of which several examples are present during just the last decade—issue new kinds of postage stamps.

Monetary changes are recorded on the stamps of that country, since the stamps are sold for use within the country and must be paid for with the currency of the land. An example of this is the "new" money of Great Britain.

All of this information is available in stamp catalogues. Not long ago, while watching a television program and listening to the characters talking about money as "rands," I was asked what country the movies was supposed to be taken in. I could not remember, so out came my Scott Stamp Catalog. Sure enough the information was there— under South Africa—the location, the government, the area of the country, the population, the capital, the politics, and lastly, the monetary system. Twelve pence equals 1 shilling, and 20 shillings equal 1 pound. Then, in 1961 the monetary system was changed to 100 cents equals 1 rand.

Such information would be very difficult to come upon, even in a large and complete encyclopedia, without much tedious research.

So you see, collecting stamps is just not a hobby of hoarding things. It is a very informative hobby, teaching the collector many things besides just the stamps themselves. In the area of color alone, stamp collecting will open your eyes to unheard-of shades, tones, and families of colors little known during the course of your daily life. There are literally dozens of wonderful colors with strange, exciting names made available for your knowledge. Artists—take note.

> Paul Villiard
> *Saugerties, N.Y.*

Acknowledgments

To Kenneth Smith of Saugerties, New York, I extend my thanks for his help in lending me his extensive stock of stamps and covers to research material to use in this book.

Thomas Gentalen of Catskill, New York, deserves special thanks for the loan of his rarities and errors for photographic purposes, especially the magnificent United States stamps shown herein.

Mr. George Putland, our local stamp dealer, also was very generous in supplying the forgeries and counterfeit stamps for me to use as examples in the chapters pertaining to that area of philately, and for the other items I found difficult to obtain when writing this volume.

To Gertrude, my wife, I owe a debt for the painstaking typing of the final manuscript, and to Dr. Thomas G. Aylesworth, my editor, for correcting my many mistakes.

Contents

Collecting Stamps
_____

Chapter One

General Information

There are a few rules to follow in the handling of stamps. The first and primary rule is never to handle a stamp in your fingers. Use tongs. Stamp tongs come in several styles. I prefer the kind called spade end. Others may prefer paddle-ended tongs, and still others the pointed end. Whatever your choice, you should never handle your stamps without using the tongs.

For many, many years, the accepted way of mounting stamps was by the use of stamp hinges. These are small rectangular pieces of gummed glassine paper, and in use the hinge is folded over a short distance from one end. This small fold is moistened with the tip of the tongue. Then the hinge is affixed to the back of the stamp right up at the top along the row of perforations. The larger portion of the hinge is then moistened, and the stamp positioned on the album page and pressed into place.

However, in recent years dealers and collectors have been objecting to stamps being hinged, and now the stamp loses value if it has had a hinge affixed. In the case of really good stamps, this devaluation may amount to a considerable sum. Most, if not all, dealers will discount 10 per cent off a stamp that has been hinged. That they do not always reduce the price proportionately when selling the stamp is another thing altogether.

So, when you purchase stamps insist on their being unhinged if you hope to have your collection increase in value, with the idea that sometime in the future it will be sold, either by you, or by your heirs. You should pay no more for an unhinged stamp than for a hinged one; but that is wishful thinking! This matter of hinging is most important in the case of mint stamps. When a stamp has been canceled, the hinge has less chance of damaging the stamp. When there is full gum on the back, sometimes the hinge will tear a layer of paper when it is removed. This is called thinning, and a thinned stamp looses nearly all its value. Unless the stamp in question is a very valuable item, it loses *all* value if thinned. A rare item may still be worth a fraction of its value, but that is all.

Besides coming in cut sizes for single stamps and blocks, these mounts are supplied in strips so you can cut to fit other sizes yourself.

For this reason it is a good practice not to hinge mint stamps but to put them in mounts of one kind or another. The best type of mount, in my estimation, is the one with a clear front and a split black back. These are made of plastic, and come in a great number of sizes to fit nearly every kind of stamp, block, plate block, and even some souvenir sheets. Select a mount that allows a small space at the edges of the stamp when it is fitted inside. This will permit the stamp to expand and contract with the weather without buckling inside the mount, as it would if the stamp fitted tightly within the edges of the plastic cover.

The backs of these mounts are gummed, and they may be mounted in albums just the same as a stamp with a hinge on the back. However, the stamp may be removed from the mount at will, replaced, or examined without damage. Other kinds of mounts are available, and some of them may appeal to you more than the split-back kind. Whatever type you select, just make sure they hold the stamp securely so the specimen does not fall out of the mount when the album pages are turned.

Actually, I no longer use albums for my stamp collection, and a great many old-timers have also given up this practice. We use stock books instead of printed albums. After you collect stamps for many years, you no longer need the printed information that usually accompanies the spaces in an album. Since to mount stamps in an album requires the use of hinges or mounts, keeping your collection in stock books is far easier and takes less time. The stamps are always free to be picked up with

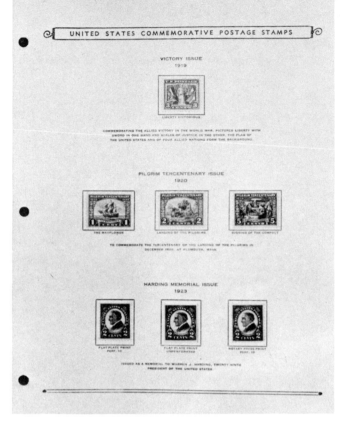

This is a White Ace page printed for United States commemorative stamps.

tongs for examination and are readily seen through the transparent pockets of the stock book.

Which brings us to the matter of what kind of stock book to use. My sincere recommendation is to use the very best kind available. The pages may be black or white. While stamps show up better against a black page, white pages are not so bad as to prohibit their use. The important factor in selecting stock books is the pocket. These should be made of clear plastic. They are usually referred to as

Here is a page from a blank loose-leaf album. The stamps show off better if lines are drawn around them in some fashion.

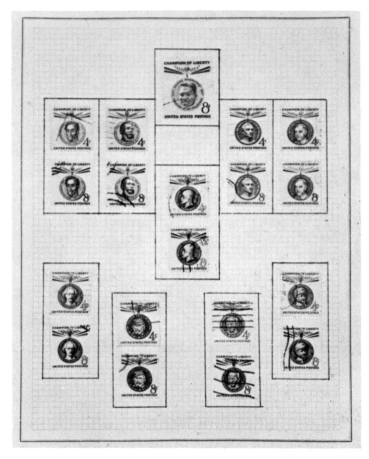

acetate pockets. Not only do acetate pockets reveal the entire stamp without hiding any part of the design or color, they hold the stamp more securely, being flat against the page and remaining so. Stock books with paper pockets are a real danger when used for holding mint stamps. The paper may soak up moisture from the air. This glues the stamp in-

A page from one of the author's stock books. The reflection is from the acetate interleaving, which protects the stamps and the pages of the book.

side the pocket, often to the extent that it cannot be removed except by running the point of your tongs along the stuck portion, thinning the specimen beyond the point of value.

Paper-pocket stock books are all right to use for canceled stamps, but since they still hide half the stamp, the acetate pockets are even better for these items. If stock books are used, the tools you need for collecting are limited to your tongs, a good magnifying glass, a perforation gauge, and a watermark detector.

For critical examination of rarities, errors, and very valuable specimens, a binocular comparison microscope is invaluable. They cost about $400 or $500 with an additional $50 to $60 for the light needed to operate it. Unless you have unlimited funds to spend on your hobby, you should not buy such an instrument. But then, unless you do have such unlimited funds, you won't be able to buy stamps so rare that they require critical examination. So it evens out to a good glass, or you might even go so far as to obtain an illuminated magnifier of one type or another.

Nearly every country in the world that has issued adhesive postage stamps has done so on special paper bearing an identifying watermark.

In order to understand just what a watermark is, one should know something about how paper is made. One method is as follows. Pulp is made by grinding up wood chips or rags or a combination of both until it is a smooth, mushy mass. When it is evenly ground to a very fine size, this pulp is mixed with water and some chemicals until it is a thick

liquid. The chemicals are used for certain purposes
—whiteners, coloring agents, hardeners to make the
paper strong. Silk threads, cut into tiny lengths and
mixed with the pulp to make it more difficult to
copy, may go into the raw pulp before it is made
into paper.

This is done on a machine having a large endless
belt of fine screening, very much like fly screening
in your windows. The pulp is fed onto the screen
through a flat nozzle the width of the screen, which
is vibrated to release the pulp in an even layer as
the screen belt passes by. The wet layer of pulp
travels on the screen across a narrow orifice connected to a suction device which sucks the water out
of the pulp, leaving it fairly dry on the screen. At
the same time, this suction pulls the pulp down
tightly against the screen, making the paper sheet
uniform in thickness.

The screen continues to travel along until the
layer of paper is picked up and fed through heated
rollers which iron out the sheet and dry it. These
are called calender rolls. From here it is rolled on
cores for storage and use.

The paper resulting from this process is an endless sheet as wide as the papermaking machine, and
as long as desired since the process is a continuous
one.

In order to put a watermark into paper, designs
are made of metal—usually brass—and these de-

A group of different watermarks showing political influence as well as the national coat of arms of Finland and the whimsical rooster of Malawi. (Watermark photos from Scott's Standard Postage Stamp Catalog. Courtesy Scott Publishing Company.)

signs are attached to the screen belt in regular positions, depending on whatever way the watermark is to be shown on the finished paper. Now, as the screen passes by the depositing nozzle, the pulp laid on the belt is thinner over the designs, due to the thickness of the material used to make them. As the paper completes the manufacturing process, this thinner area remains in the pulp, and in the finished paper it results in a much thinner area. When the paper is held to the light, one can readily see these thin spots.

However, after the paper has been used to print postage stamps, the watermark may be hidden by the dark ink evenly applied to the surface of the paper. In order to detect the watermark in this case, the stamp is placed in a black dish of some kind and covered with benzene or lighter fluid. Small black-glass dishes are sold as watermark detectors, and these are commonly used for the detection of the thinned designs. As soon as the stamp is wetted thoroughly with the volatile fluid, the thin areas of a watermark stand out quite plainly against the black background of the dish. The benzene does not affect the inks used in printing stamps, nor does it effect the gum on mint stamps. The stamp may be laid on a clean cloth or in a drying book, after detecting the watermark, and allowed to dry, which takes only a few minutes as a general rule.

Watermarks are a very important method of identification and for separating varieties in the same

A block of stamps in a watermark detector. The reflections are from the fluid in the black glass, but the watermark is clearly visible.

stamp. Sometimes an issue is reprinted on paper without the same watermark as the first issue. Sometimes the reprint lacks a watermark, or if the first issue was not on watermarked paper, perhaps the second was. There are infinite varieties possible in printing stamps.

As a rule, the United States stamps are printed on unwatermarked paper, although in the earlier issues paper was used with a watermark USPS repeated all over the sheet. Revenue stamps were printed on paper bearing the watermark USIR in repeated lines.

In 1938 the dollar value of the definitive postage set of Presidents was in error, printed on this USIR paper. The stamp had originally been printed on the regular unwatermarked paper, until it was required to reprint some. This is when the error occurred, and today the error is worth a great deal of money. The story goes that a stamp collector who was watermarking an assortment of stamps for identification accidently dropped one of the United States $1.00 stamps into the watermark dish and, lo and behold, the watermark showed up bright and strong. I cannot attest to the veracity of this story, but it seems reasonable that the watermark error *was* discovered by accident because there would be no real reason to put United States stamps through a watermark detector, since we do not normally use watermarked paper.

Throughout the years watermarking paper has shown an interesting picture of the development of different countries. Some countries use paper watermarked with political significance. Others with emblems designed to promote national pride—as the coat of arms of that country. Others use watermark designs pertaining to industry or commerce, while some just use a design which they fancy to identify their stamps.

In the early days in the United States, the stamps were printed by private printing companies. The government farmed out their stamp and money work to these individual firms. More recently, however, the Bureau of Printing and Engraving took over all the paper money and stamp printing.

Stamps used to be printed in two ways—flat-plate

printing and rotary-press printing. We now have a third method—the Giori-press printings. In the case of mint stamps it is very easy to tell at a glance if the stamp is flat plate or rotary press. Since often the same stamp was printed in both fashions, and since usually one or the other increases in value over the opposite variety, it is necessary to be able to tell them apart.

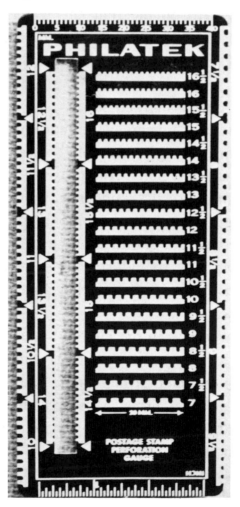

A perforation gauge is necessary to identify varieties in perforations. Metal ones are better than plastic ones.

If the stamp is unused, turn it over and look at the back. The paper and gum will show a series of even ripples clear across the stamp if it is printed on the rotary press. The stamp and gum will be perfectly flat and without waves of any kind if it was flat plate. In the case of a canceled stamp, it is a bit more difficult to tell which is which. This can only be done by measurement, either of the stamp itself or of the perforations. Sometimes, both. Usually the rotary-press printings are slightly larger than the flat-plate printings in one direction. These dimensions are given in stamp catalogues for your guidance. Sometimes the perforations on rotary-press stamps are different in one or in both directions from those of the flat-plate stamps.

Both of these differences can be measured with the aid of a simple device known as a perforation gauge. This is a metal plate having perforations marked on it of all the different sizes used in the manufacture of stamps. In addition, it has a short metric scale and a short regular rule to use in measuring the sizes of stamps. To use, you merely match the perforations of a stamp with those on the gauge. When you come across the one that exactly covers the stamp, the size is read directly on the scale. Again, perforations are indicated in stamp catalogues, and the gauge is used to check only when a stamp is issued with more than one type of perforation.

As a general rule, stamps of the United States are not invalidated after a given time. Stamps can be used for postage many, many years after they are no longer sold in the post office, and as a matter of fact, a stamp that may be worth many dollars as a collector's item, may still be used on a letter for exactly the amount of its face value. Needless to say, this would be rather foolish to do, but the idea is, it can be done.

Certain stamps are invalidated for the simple reason that the service for which they were issued is no longer offered by the post office. The beautiful set of parcel post stamps, and the set of special-handling stamps are no longer useful as postage, nor are the parcel post postage-due stamps.

Most other countries invalidate their stamps after a given period of time. This is especially true of the countries that have or have had drastic changes in their currency. Germany is especially noted for that. After the First World War the value of German money dropped to a fantastically unbelievable low, and this is reflected in their stamps. The currency was the pfennig and the mark. One hundred pfennigs made a mark.

Then came the crash. Where stamps had been issued in 1-pfennig values upward, and a 1-pfennig stamp would carry a post card, the stamp values rose until they were issued in mark values. The mark continued to drop. Soon stamps required to

The cost of postage rose from 1 pfennig to 20 billion marks during the 1920s.

post a letter called for the value of hundreds of *marks* instead of 2 or 3 pfennigs. The hundreds of marks soon rose again until it took a stamp valued at several thousands of marks. Then again to hundreds of thousands of marks for a stamp to mail a letter. As time went on, the values rose to the millions, and as though there was no end in sight as to the depths the country's money could drop, finally the values of a single stamp to mail a simple letter rose to several *billions* of marks.

People in this country are constantly bemoaning the fact that our dollar is practically worthless. Can you imagine how a German person felt when his country's money fell so far? Where before he could buy a package of cigarettes or a candy bar for 10 or 15 pfennigs, he would now have to pay anywhere from 50 billion to 100 billion marks for the same purchase! Some drop!

The government life insurance stamps of New Zealand are unique, and some of them are very beautiful. In 1869 the New Zealand Government Life Insurance Office was formed, and an arrangement was made with the postal department for the Life Insurance Office to issue its own stamps. These were first issued in 1891. Appropriately, the illustrations on the first issue, as well as on all subsequent issues, were various lighthouses.

These stamps would make an ideal topical collection, and, indeed, many persons do collect them as topicals of lighthouses. The coasts of New Zealand were rugged and treacherous, and the scene of many marine disasters. Lighthouses are placed in many strategic positions, and these, as well as other lighthouses throughout the British Empire, are depicted on the insurance stamps.

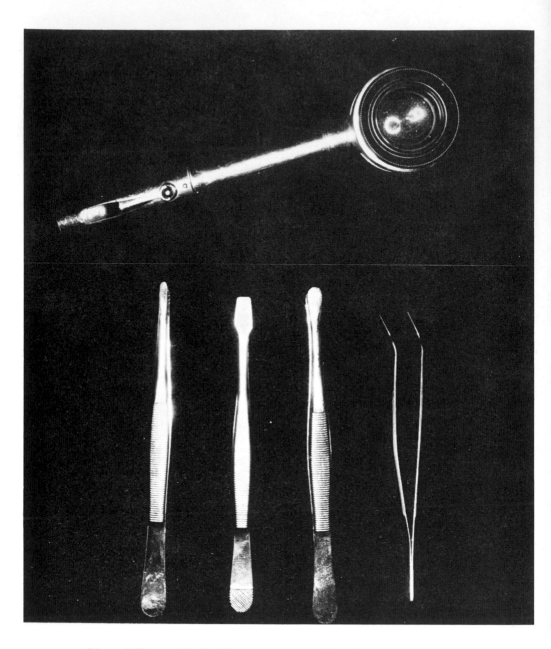

Four different kinds of tongs and an illuminated magnifier for use in handling a stamp collection.

Chapter Two

The Care and Handling of Stamps

Many collections of postage stamps, which if properly treated would be valuable, are, instead, merely accumulations worth practically nothing because of improper handling.

Perhaps the greatest sin of mishandling a stamp is to handle it with your fingers. I cannot emphasize enough the most important point that stamps should *never* be handled except with a pair of fine stamp tongs. These are available in three main designs—all depending upon the shape of the points. The professional and dealer usually use tongs with fairly sharp points. They are used because these tongs can be used to roll a hinge off a stamp without tearing or thinning the stamp—provided, of course, that the hinge used was one of the peelable variety. Some of the older hinges were not peelable, and taking them off the stamp with a pair of tongs is merely inviting trouble.

If the stamp is mint, then nothing can be done except, perhaps, to cut the loose flap of the hinge off carefully, leaving the glued part still stuck to the stamp. If the stamp is canceled, then the chances are you can resoak the stamp and remove the hinge that way. Be careful to wipe off the hinge gum while the stamp is wet and soaking, otherwise it may dry as a square of gum on the back of an otherwise ungummed stamp, causing a shrinking or curl at that point, which may ruin the stamp.

The tong shape most handy for beginners, and advanced collectors as well, especially if they are not using hinges to mount their specimens, is the spade point. This tool has a squarish, shovel or spadelike shape at the points which afford the maximum amount of support to the stamp. The trouble with most spade-point tongs is the thickness of the points. In order to be useful, the points should be as thin as possible. I have overcome the trouble by grinding down the points of my spade tongs carefully until they are paper-thin at the ends.

An intermediate kind is called paddle-pointed. This variety has small round paddle-shaped points, usually much thinner than the spade points and quite a bit smaller. Some companies sell very fine tongs, for double or more the usual cost of the tool. These have very thin points, and are gold-plated to prevent corrosion and rust.

I might mention here that tongs are not used to handle stamps when soaking them off paper. This is the only time when stamps are handled with the fingers. If you used tongs on wet stamps, and the tongs had been used until the plating was worn off the points, there is a good possibility that the steel would leave a mark on the wet stamp that would later turn into a rust stain impossible to remove. Since the stamp is soft, limp, and wet, it can be handled with the fingers without any danger of leaving oil stains from your hand. As soon as it is dry, however, break out the tongs to handle it.

When soaking stamps off pieces of paper or the envelope on which they were used, they should be left in the water only long enough to entirely soften and dissolve the gum. Further soaking will do nothing toward releasing the stamp from the paper, but it is very possible to ruin the stamp if it is next to another on which an aniline dye was used in the printing. This dye could bleed from one stamp to another, ruining both in the process.

Stamps on brown wrapping paper should never be soaked together with stamps on ordinary white-envelope stock. The brown paper, especially the corrugated cardboard used in making cartons, will often color the soaking water and stain the stamps.

As a matter of fact, if the stamps can be removed by methods other than soaking, it is far better to do so.

There is a medium on the market today that is said to remove stamps from paper without soaking them. The use of this medium would obviate staining and save stamps otherwise ruined by the color from brown paper. This is called Magic Stamp Release, and small bottles can be purchased from any stamp dealer or from stamp departments in larger stores. Care should be used in removing stamps with this fluid because here, too, aniline-dye printed stamps may run or stain. If possible, test the liquid on a reject or damaged stamp before using it on your good specimens.

Another thing to watch out for is foreign air mail envelopes. Most foreign envelopes are made of very thin paper, with the inside printed with a dark blue dye to make them opaque. This dye can be murder when you soak off stamps, producing a dish of blue soup that stains every stamp in it to the point of ruination. Try soaking them off one stamp at a time in individual dishes, to make sure that the dye does not stain any other stamps, and soak them only long enough to loosen the stamp, removing it as soon as it can be peeled from the piece of paper. Perhaps the Magic Stamp Release would be of value in removing these kinds of specimens.

While clean towels are good for drying soaked-off stamps, a drying book is better.

After the stamps have been soaked off the paper, they must be dried before they can be put away in stock books or mounted in albums. The drying can be accomplished by laying out the wet stamps in rows on a clean terry-cloth towel, covering them with another towel and laying a weight, such as a book, on top to keep the stamps flat. Don't let the stamps touch each other. Take care when laying the covering towel in place that you do not move the stamps, causing them to overlap one another or even folding over a corner. A crease put into a stamp this way can never be removed.

A far better method of drying soaked stamps is to use a drying book. These are sold by stamp dealers for a couple of dollars and can be used over and over and will last many years. They are merely books with pages of heavy blotting paper, and the stamps are placed on the last page first, the next page turned to cover them, then the pages continuing to be loaded and covered until the book is filled or until you have positioned all your stamps. The book is then laid flat and a book or other weight placed on top. Let the whole thing stand for a day or two to insure that the stamps are entirely dry. If all the gum was removed in the soaking water, there is no danger of the stamps sticking to the blotter pages.

After the stamps are dry, they should be carefully examined for tears, creases, missing perforations, thin spots, and any other damage which may be present. Any stamp having any damage whatever should be separated from the others and filed away by itself. You might keep a special stock book in which damaged stamps are placed. Of course, if the damage is at all severe, the only thing to do is throw the stamp in the wastebasket. Slight damages, however, still may leave the stamp usable as trading stock for very beginners, who can put it in their album as a space filler and later, perhaps, replace it with a perfect copy. Whenever trading or selling such a stamp you should very carefully point out the damage to your prospective customer, to make absolutely certain he is not trading or buying under the false impression of getting a good stamp.

Often you will see listed by some dealer or other, stamps called *repaired*. These are damaged stamps that have been fixed up in some way to hide the damage. Since this is a lot of work and takes skill and time to do properly, such stamps are usually valuable items, well worth the time and trouble. A tiny tear, for example, can be glued in place under a magnifying glass, to the point where it is practically invisible. Still, the stamp is damaged and should be listed as such.

Another very important point in the care and handling of a stamp collection is the storage of the albums or stock books. These should never be stored on their edges or ends unless you have enough books to wedge them tightly into a shelf space so the pages will be held pressed together. Rather, albums and stock books are best laid flat on their sides, preferably with another book (perhaps your stamp catalogues) laid on top of the pile to hold the pages together.

Dampness is the bane of stamp collections, and many a fine and valuable stamp has been ruined or, at best, most of its value lost by becoming glued to the album page during a spell of hot, humid weather. In nearly every case, you will find that the album had been stored loosely with the pages open, or at least not pressed together. This permits air to enter the book between the pages. In humid weather the air carries a great amount of moisture, and the gum on the backs of mint stamps is *intended* to soak up moisture to adhere it to the envelope. It will adhere as readily to the album page!

Under certain conditions, stamps so stuck to pages can be removed without damage to the gum. Sometimes the gum will be disfigured in some way, which—true—will drop the value of the stamp, but at least it will not be entirely worthless. Very thin spade-pointed tongs may be slid underneath the stamp and worked slowly and carefully to loosen it. This can also thin the stamp without you knowing it. Sometimes heating the tongs gently before sliding them under the stamp will help.

If the stamp is stuck to glassine pages, as would be the case in a mint-sheet album, for example, they may sometimes peel off easily by rolling the page away from the stamps. If they are stuck really tightly, do not make an attempt to peel them off, because you will almost surely thin the stamps. In this case, placing the stuck stamps in a freezer overnight may help. The principle is the same as freeze-drying of foods, the freezing cold removing all the moisture from the gum, permitting the stamps to snap off the paper they were stuck to.

However, there is another danger connected with freeze-releasing of stamps. When the stamps are removed from the freezer, they warm up rapidly, the warming process causing them to sweat, due to their soaking up moisture from the air. If you take them from the freezer and put them immediately into your stock books, the chances are that you will really glue them fast. They should be put face up on a towel or in a blotter drying book until they have equalized in temperature, at which time they may be remounted. There is a possibility that stamps so treated will curl as they warm up, but this is not really a great problem, especially if you use stock books instead of albums where the stamps are hinge mounted. Merely slide the stamp into the stock pocket and it will flatten out all by itself. Make no attempt to flatten the stamp by drawing it over a straight edge or any other object. You may scrape off some of the ink if the stamp is engraved, or some of the design if it is printed in offset.

Since stamp values are predicated almost entirely on the condition of the item, great care should be exercised in handling the stamp not to damage the perforations. Just one perforation, broken from the stamp, or even torn just enough to shorten it, will cause a dealer, when appraising the stamp with intent to purchase it, to lower the value a large percentage.

By now you must be getting the idea that if you

sneeze while looking at your stamp collection, the value will drop. *Everything* makes the price go down. This is exactly the idea I want to get across, since most beginning stamp collectors, and many experienced ones, have no idea of the tiny things dealers will pick on to reduce the price they will pay for a collection.

To get back to the perforations—when stamps are separated from each other, they should never simply be pulled apart. First they should be carefully creased down the line of perforations. This puts a crease down the *middle* of the perforations, permitting the stamps to be separated with an equal amount of perforation remaining on both stamps. This evenness is most important. If one or more perforations are pulled crookedly, they will be long on one stamp and short on the other. The stamp with the long perforations is all right, because the perforations can be trimmed and the stamp remain with its full percentage of length. The other stamp, however, has lost a large amount of its value, because the perforations cannot be made their proper length again.

Perforations may also be damaged when mounting the stamp. If hinges are placed on the stamp for album mounting and the hinge is glued to the stamp over the perforations, then they will almost surely tear off when the hinge is removed. If, on the other hand, the hinge is placed too low down on the stamp, when the stamp is lifted for examination the perforations will crease across the top, causing damage that is difficult or impossible to correct. The hinge should be moistened on the bottom edge of the flap, but placed with the top edge of the crease in the hinge at the top edge of the perforations. In this fashion, the stamp is supported by the hinge, but the perforations are left free and unglued to the hinge.

If stamps are kept in stock books, there is danger of creasing or even tearing off a perforation when slipping the stamp into the page pocket. This is also a danger when using the Lindner hingeless album pages. Take care to make certain that the stamp is inserted in the pocket with the pocket held up off the stamp until the entire bottom edge of the stamp is below the edge of the pocket. The stamp may now be slid into place without danger of damaging the perforations. Two pairs of tongs, one holding the pocket open and the other holding the stamp, may be used, or you can pick up the pocket edge with the tongs, then hold it up with your fingernail while you slide the stamp in place.

If you are a block collector, care must also be taken of the perforations between the stamps in the block. If a block is creased along the perforations, it no longer has value as a block but only as four individual stamps, except in the case of very rare and costly items which even then drop in value for the creased perforations.

The entire policy in collecting stamps is to keep

them in perfect, immaculate, mint condition at all times, protecting them from any possible kind of damage, either from the elements or from handling them.

A collection should be "worked" regularly. Stamps mounted in albums should be gone through every couple of months at the very latest. This means that each stamp should be examined individually. If hinge mounted, the stamp should be picked up on the hinge to make certain it has not been stuck to the page. Also, any incorrectly mounted stamp should be removed and remounted. It is surprising, even when you take great care in mounting your stamps originally, to see how many can be better mounted after examination at a later date. Time and again, as you go over your collection, a stamp mounted crookedly or improperly will catch your eye.

Surplus stamps can be kept in stock books, or in small glassine envelopes in a card file box if preferred. Stock books are by far the best way to hold your surplus. After any spell of hot, humid weather, both your collection and your surplus stock should be gone over. This applies only to mint stamps, of course, because canceled stamps, unless they are the canceled-to-order variety—which still have full gum —will not stick together. If you store your surplus stamps in glassine envelopes, they should be removed from the envelope, separated, then returned to the envelope. This should be done, not during the humid spell, but a couple of days after it is over. Working stamps during humid weather merely adds to the difficulty, since each stamp is then exposed to the dampness in the air.

Chapter Three

Symbols Used in Philately

Many abbreviations are used in describing stamps in dealer's lists, auction lists, and in catalogues. Some of these abbreviations may be unfamiliar to a beginner, who would not know what the dealer was trying to say. Many symbols are used, too, in stamp newspapers, to denote blocks, covers, etc., but for the most part these and their explanations are listed at the tops of the ads, and the reader can tell from the key what they mean.

I will list here some of the more commonly used abbreviations, taken from many dealers' and auctioneers' ads, and from catalogues. They may help in identifying a stamp.

Avg.—*Average condition*

blk—*Block of stamps (usually a block of four unless otherwise specified)*

C—*Canceled (used) stamp*

cr—*Creased stamp*

CTO—*Canceled to order*

F—*Fine condition*

FDC—*First day cover*

FFC—*First flight cover*

G—*Good condition*

hh—*Heavily hinged copy*

hpr—*Horizontal pair of coil stamps (or other stamps)*

HR—*Hinge remnants still on the stamp*

LH—*Lightly hinged stamp*

lpr—*Line pair—usually pertaining to coil stamps*

M—*Mint (unused) stamp*

NH—*Never hinged stamp*

OC—*On cover*

OG—*Original gum*

O.pce—*On piece—usually refers to a stamp on a piece of cover.*

Pbl, or P⌗b1, or PB—*Plate-number block*

Pbl/LL—*Lower left-hand plate-number block*

Pbl/LR—*Lower right-hand plate-number block*

Pbl/UL—*Upper left-hand plate-number block*

Pbl/UR—*Upper right-hand plate-number block*

Perf.—*Perforated*

Ps, or P⌗s—*Plate-number single*

Pr, or POOR—*Poorly conditioned stamp*

Ps/UR, Ps/LR, Ps/LL—*Apply to the positions in plate-number singles.*

s—*Single stamp*

se, or st/e—*Straight-edged stamp*

sm.flts—*Minor faults, or minor damage to stamp*

S/S—*Souvenir sheet*

st—*Stained specimen*

T—*Thinned (damaged stamp)*

tt, or sth—*Small thinned spot on stamp*

U—*Used stamp*

Uh—*Unhinged*

unwmkd—*Unwatermarked*

v—*Values (i.e., 12v means there are 12 stamps of different values in a set)*

VF—*Very fine condition*

VG—*Very good condition (slightly less than VF condition)*

vpr—*Vertical pair—usually pertaining to coil stamps.*

Wmk, or wmk—*Watermark*

*-x—*Mint stamp, but without gum*

Sometimes numbers are placed after an abbreviation, as: Pbl/6. This means that the plate-number block consists of six stamps in place of the usual four. Plate-number blocks of flat-bed printings are collected in sixes. Often you will see a listing, especially in dealers lists or auction lists, like Pce22. The dealer is offering a piece, or part of a sheet, consisting of twenty-two stamps. He will not break up the piece, but wishes to sell it intact, letting the purchaser do what he wants as far as breaking it down into smaller pieces.

A block of four early air mail stamps. All perforations must be intact and unseparated for collection purposes.

Chapter Four

Ways to Collect Stamps

When stamp collecting began, "way back in the old days," collections consisted of stamps taken from envelopes that had gone through the mails. The stamps were either removed from the envelopes or left intact with the complete cover. Soon, however, stamp collecting began to break up into specialized divisions. Today, it is hard to find any branch of stamp collecting that is not practiced either as a part of a general collection or by itself. First day covers—the stamp placed by a postmaster, on the first day it is on sale, on an addressed envelope sent to him by you, then canceled with a special cachet—is an important special collecting practice.

The four positions of a regular plate-number block.

Many persons like to collect stamps in blocks of four. Some like to collect blocks, but with the plate numbers on them. Usually a block of four has a value of five of the same stamp in single condition, and a plate-number block the value of six regular stamps. There are, naturally, exceptions to this valuation, and some stamps worth, for example, $5.00 for a single specimen, may have a value of $50 or $100 or even more as a plate block. This depends, naturally, upon the stamp—whether it is so rare that the chance of a plate block being in existence is practically nil.

In the sheets of stamps printed in the United States, for example, the stamps are in four panes of fifty or one hundred or more or less, as the case may be, separated by a wide gutter between the panes. The panes are cut apart after printing, to the individual "sheets" as sold in the post office. The plate numbers, zip code inscriptions, and any other inscription on the margin of the sheets will occur on the upper left, upper right, lower left, and lower right positions on different sheets. Position-blocks collecting, therefore, indicates that blocks having the plate number in all four positions are desired to complete the selection of that particular specimen. Position collecting has been further re-fined to the collecting of the four positions of each separate plate number used in printing that issue. This can run into a lot of money and a lot of storage space after a while.

Since the advent of the enormous complicated printing presses imported from foreign countries to print multicolored postage, a new turn has taken place in plate-number block collecting. First of all, we have begun to print *se-tenant* stamps. This means that the sheet (pane) purchased in the post office contains either two or four different stamps printed next to one another on the same sheet. In the case of the recent flag issue, ten different stamps occu-pied *se-tenant* positions in the same pane.

Since the pane is one corner of the full printing sheet, and the sheet contains four plate numbers at its four corners, it stands to reason that each plate number position will be next to a different stamp in the block of four usually designated as the quantity to go with the number. Hence, every specializing collector must collect *four* plate blocks of each *se-tenant* stamp, instead of only one, in order to have the complete available set for that particular issue. (I am not including the collection of different plate numbers. That is carrying the specialization to its extreme limit.)

Since each plate-number block collector tries to get four position blocks of the *se-tenant* stamps, this means that the demand for such stamps is four times as great as the demand for regularly printed stamps. To think a little further, this also means that for an investment collector *se-tenant* issues should be good, since the demand will exceed the normal supply four times faster than usual. So, for you who wish to collect as an investment for future profits, *se-tenant* United States postage looks like a good bet. You might put a sheet or two aside in a good protective album and forget about them for a few years. You may be in for a very pleasant surprise.

Somewhere back along the line someone decided that the way to collect plate-number blocks was as four stamps for regular issues printed on the rotary

Two plate-number blocks in which the plate numbers are in unusual positions. This occurs mostly on multicolored stamps having several plates.

presses, and six stamps for issues printed on the flat-bed presses. Now comes the Giori press from Italy capable of turning out works of art in many different colors.

Since each color requires a different plate to print it from, and since each plate is numbered in order to keep track of it, some of the recent issues of stamps have as many as eight or ten plate numbers on each pane. This means that a plate-number block of such issues must contain from six to twenty stamps in order to comply with the accepted method of collecting. A plate-number block that does not have the entire set of plate numbers on it is not considered a plate-number block at all, but merely a block of stamps. So when you get a new issue take care to examine the sheet in the post office before you buy it, and determine how many stamps must be kept intact in order to make an accepted plate-number block.

To digress for just a moment, the Cape Hatteras stamp recently issued as part of the National Parks Centennial set requires that eight stamps be attached in order to make up a "Mail Early in the Day" block. More about this stamp later.

In the *se-tenant* stamps of the United States, we have issued sheets containing two stamps *se-tenant*, and several kinds with four *se-tenant* specimens. Notable among the paired stamps is the issue of Space Achievement and Space Walk, the latter

A zip block of *se-tenant* **stamps. The zip inscription and the plate numbers will fall opposite a different stamp in each position.**

showing an astronaut walking in space attached to his spaceship by an umbilical hose. This stamp has risen to a very high value—one recent listing I have seen quotes $13.95 for the plate-number block of four, although I am certain that the block can be had for several dollars under that figure. The point is, the stamp is rising rapidly in price, and stocks are increasingly hard to find. I imagine it will continue to go up until it reaches a very high level, then, as collectors and investors unload their stocks for the purpose of realizing a high return for their investment, the price will drop to a more realistic figure, finally steadying out—but still at a nice

Three different styles of the zip inscription.

profit over the original cost of 5 cents per stamp, or $2.50 for a pane of fifty. It is now priced at $88 per pane!

Besides plate-number blocks, the blocks containing the advertisement for using the zip code on the margin and the block containing the advertisement for mailing early in the day are collectable items. The Mail Early blocks are always collected as blocks of six stamps, with the tab margin containing the inscription opposite the middle stamp in the

The three different blocks that are collectable from a pane of stamps. "Mail Early" blocks are always of six stamps.

block. The exception is the Cape Hatteras stamp
mentioned earlier in this chapter, which must be a
block of eight stamps with the inscription off-center
in the margin.

The reason for this abberation is that the Cape
Hatteras stamp is the very first composite stamp this
country has ever issued. It is the lowest denomination of the five-stamp set commemorating the National Parks Centennial.

It is issued in panes of one hundred 2-cent
stamps, four of which together make a picture of
the national beach at Cape Hatteras. The four
stamps are designed within a single frame and perforated to separate into single 2-cent stamps, each
bearing one fourth of the design. The four together,
make an 8-cent stamp, which at the time of issue is
the standard postal rate for letters. This, beside the
fact that it is the first composite stamp issued by
the United States, will serve to increase its value,
in my opinion, because four of them are needed to
make a letter-rate stamp; four are needed to complete the design, and four plate-number blocks total-
ing sixteen stamps are required to make a complete
plate-number arrangement, since each position of
the plate number will fall on a different stamp in
the same design.

The sheet of this stamp, when intact, is beautiful.
It clearly shows a pane of twenty-five complete pictures, each with the value of 8 cents. On close in-

The first composite stamp the United States has ever issued. Four 2-cent stamps, making one 8-cent complete picture. This should rise in value.

spection the perforating can be seen, and the pane is noted to be indeed a sheet of one hundred 2-cent stamps. A novel idea for our government, and more than likely one that will be repeated in time to come.

European stamps have long been issued in (to us) odd printings. Small sheets are commonplace and are often mistaken for souvenir sheets, when in reality they are not. East Germany issues stamps in miniature sheets of six denominations. These are printed in large sheets of the sets, then cut apart to make the miniature sheets. Often, too, they print their stamps in adjacent groups of several different denominations and colors, breaking the large sheet up into individual groups perforated all around but without the gutter margins at the edges.

West Germany also printed several kinds of

A *tête-bêche* pair, and a second pair separated to show that, parted, they become two regular stamps. To be *tête-bêche* the pair must be intact.

stamps in very large sheets, half the sheet (divided vertically) with the stamp in the normal position, and the other half with the design upside down. There was no gutter between the two sides of the sheet, making the two stamps next to each other fall into the *tête-bêche* category.

Ordinarily, *tête-bêche* stamps occur in plates made up of many individually transferred designs, when one transfer is made upside down in error. This would make only one *tête-bêche* pair occur in each sheet, and these two stamps could be called errors, so the price is accordingly high. In the case of the German printings, however, the stamps, while actually *tête-bêche,* are not so because of errors in the making of the plates, and they may be purchased at the regular low price of a pair of the stamps or, at most, a very small premium.

Collecting single stamps is still the most popular way of building up your hobby, and here you have the choice of two ways—mint or used. Sometimes you can use a combination of the two, collecting special countries in mint condition, and the rest of the world in used specimens. Many collectors make their foreign collection in used and United States in mint because of the steady value of United States mint stamps.

A collector must be ready to pay a 10 per cent premium for stamps never hinged, or to take a similar loss in selling stamps that have been hinged. To combat this loss of value, it is a good idea not to hinge your mint stamps but to keep them either in special albums having individual pockets for stamps or in stock books where they do not need any support to hold them in place. Albums are made in Switzerland that have spaces for all individual stamps, but not for hinging. Each space is a built-in clear plastic pocket into which the stamp is slipped, being removable any time you wish to examine it.

Other than this type of album, a collection of

mint stamps could be kept in stock books having the pockets made of clear plastic, which does not hide any of the stamp. This is the way I prefer to keep stamps since they are maintained flat and protected, are readily accessible at all times, and the stock book pages are easy to turn and lie flat while you are looking at your collection.

Collecting single stamps can be broken down into more categories than just mint or used. You can collect only one country, attempting to make a collection complete by having a specimen of every stamp that country ever issued. Or, you can collect a group of a country and its colonies. For example, perhaps the most popular collections of this type are of British colonies and Great Britain. In a way, this almost amounts to a world-wide collection since, as the British used to say, "The sun never

Meter stamps are also collected by specialists. They are usually affixed to parcel post by the postal clerks.

The tabs intact on Israeli stamps increase the value, sometimes greatly.

sets on the British Empire." This was literally true since Britain had colonies in every part of the world, and whenever Great Britain issued a special commemorative stamp, she usually did so for her entire nation. That meant one or more stamps for each and every colony, as well as for the mother country.

Belgium and its colonies is another popular group, as is the Netherlands and its colonies. As a matter of fact, Benelux countries are often grouped and collected as one. Benelux is the combined abbreviation for Belgium, the Netherlands, and Luxembourg. Special albums are available for Benelux collections.

Another pair of very popular countries for specialized collecting are Germany and Russia. At the time of writing this book, Japan is just beginning to become popular and, while right now stamps of the Ryukyu Islands are not too costly, I predict that these stamps are going to jump in value to a great degree, and it might be a good country to consider for investment while the stamps are low-priced. The stamps should be purchased in never-hinged, unused condition, and you should insist that they be not less than very fine specimens. Otherwise, when you go to sell them, the dealers will discount part of the price for the centering if it is less than VF.

Some countries, notably Israel, issue their stamps in sheets of small numbers, and along the bottom edge of each sheet are printed tabs carrying a legend of some kind. These tabs are perforated so they may be removed from the stamp, but usually the bottom stamp with the tab attached is held at greater value than the stamp without the tab. If you collect stamps especially for their increase in value, then when purchasing new issues you should always buy tabbed specimens rather than plain stamps, since almost invariably if the stamp does increase in value in a few years, the tabbed specimen will be worth several times the amount of the plain stamp. Usually tab stamps are collected unused, but there are used copies available as well. While other countries do not make a steady practice of printing their stamps in tabbed sheets, still a great number of countries have issued stamps with a tab of some kind attached to them.

Topical collecting is very popular, and there

The tabs on these Belgian stamps are printed in French and Flemish. Freely translated, they say, "No delivery on Sunday."

seems to be no limit to the number of topics available on the stamps of the world. Topical collecting merely means that you collect stamps having to do with some specific thing. For example, music on stamps is a topic that is most popular. This topical

Music topicals may show just the music, the composer, or an instrument. All would be included in a music collection.

**Topical stamps may be collected showing anything imagi-
nable: maps, ships, masks, famous people, jewelry, insects—
you name it.**

selection may be further broken down into actual
musical notes shown on stamps, musical instru-
ments pictured, or the musicians themselves. Still
finer divisions may be made by collecting stamps
picturing only composers or only musical artists.

Birds, animals, reptiles, mammals—or a specific mammal, such as horses or monkeys or almost any mammal you can think of—one country or another is sure to have printed a stamp with the animal you wish depicted on it. Flowers are popular, and these again may be divided into wild flowers, cultivated flowers, orchids, etc.

Buildings, ships, famous people, Presidents, children, maps, flags—you have your pick of literally dozens of topics around which to build an excellent collection.

There are dealers throughout the country specializing in topical stamps, and they offer a service in topicals as they are issued. You subscribe to the service, and they either notify you or send you the stamps as they come out. This way you are made aware of the topicals you want to collect as they are printed, and you do not miss any countries that might otherwise escape your notice.

Olympic games stamps are a good topic to collect, and many countries have issued stamps commemorating the different Olympics throughout the years. To commemorate the 1972 Olympic games, the United States issued a 6-cent, an 8-cent, a 15-cent, and an 11-cent air mail stamp. Two were in commemoration of the winter Olympics held in Sapporo, Japan, and the other two for the games held in Munich, West Germany. Many other countries have also issued stamps for this occasion.

Chapter Five

Booklet Panes and Coil Stamps

Booklet stamps have been in use in this country since 1900. They are convenient, easy to carry around in your wallet or purse, and they are made up in several different denominations, including air mail.

For the most part, booklet panes are not too expensive, although some of the very early panes do run up into a high-priced category. For example, the panes from booklets issued for use by the American Expeditionary Force in Europe are very high in cost today. These panes were of thirty stamps instead of the usual six or eight stamps in use today.

In printing stamps for booklet panes, a slightly

A regular booklet of stamps, "exploded," and one of the test gum booklets.

different positioning is used from that of the normal postage. A typical rotary-press plate, for example, carries three hundred and twenty impressions, making forty panes of eight stamps each. Every fourth vertical row has a wider space between the impressions, and there is also a wide space running horizontally across the center of the sheet. The stamps are perforated completely, vertically, but only between every other row, horizontally, the panes being cut apart in the imperforated rows.

Recently the postal service issued booklets of 6-cent stamps coated with a matte gum, which, being non-hygroscopic, did not need the interleaving, as did booklet stamps to date. This type of gum, if successful, would save a considerable amount of time, labor, and material, dispensing with the interleaving of booklets.

However, the postal rate changed to 8 cents shortly after the test-gum booklets were issued, and these were issued with the regular gum. This meant that the test-gum booklets were immediately a collector's item, being in very short supply, and the price went up accordingly.

It is not conceivable that the postal service was unaware that the rate was going to change, and why they issued a special booklet the way they did is beyond understanding. However, they did, and so created another variety for the many philatelists who collect such items.

Now this matte gum is standard on our booklet panes of stamps, except I note that air mail booklets are still being issued with the regular gum. In time, I suppose these, too, will carry the non-stick gum, and maybe we will even issue our regular sheet stamps with the new gum.

It might be better if we did, since the matte gum does not seem to curl as does the gum we have been using all these years. And, certainly in damp weather, the matte gum does not soak up moisture, causing the sheets to stick in their albums.

Combination booklets are issued, having eight 11-cent air mail stamps in two panes of four stamps and two labels, and one pane of six regular 2-cent stamps. The booklet is priced at $1.00 and is somewhat smaller than the regular booklets. On the panes of air mail stamps, one label is "Mail Early in the Day," and the other is devoted to the zip code inscription. The 2-cent pane carries no labels.

On the latest 8-cent regular postage booklets selling for $2.00, the top cover carries the denomination and price, the inside having a facsimile addressed envelope to show how it should be written. However, on the outside of the back cover is a slogan, "Collect your nation's postage stamps: miniatures of American history," together with the replica of the two Space Achievement stamps in *se-tenant* attachment.

The panes within the booklet are: one pane of four stamps with two extra large labels, one announcing the matte gum being used, and the other telling the contents and price of the booklet. Two other panes have seven stamps each, and a zip code label, and the last pane has seven stamps and the "Mail Early in the Day" label.

Booklet panes should be collected intact, and the staples holding the booklets together very carefully removed so as not to tear the individual panes. Booklet panes lacking the staple holes have a large premium placed on their value.

All booklet pane stamps have at least one

Imperforate errors of the regular 10-cent air mail coil stamp are very valuable. They must be collected as an intact pair.

straight edge. Some have two, when they fall on the corners of the panes. This identifies single stamps as coming from booklet panes if the design and color is the same as that of a regular issue stamp.

In the United States, coil stamps often contain rare items or errors. I say often contain. What I really meant to say was that in the *past* they often contained such irregularities. Not so many in later years since better controls and more precise machines are used to produce them. Some of the errors or, to be more exact, varieties to be found in older coils were paste-ups and folded-paper printings. Paste-up denoted a stamp that was printed over that part of the paper roll that was pasted together to form a continuous strip during the printing process. When a roll of paper was about to run out in the presses, a new roll was pasted to the edge of the old, permitting continuous printing without having to reload the press.

The stamps printed over this joint were held at a higher premium than the normal stamps in the coil. Although folded-paper varieties were more often found in sheet stamps than coils, they were also found in the latter. They occurred when the paper accidently became folded as it fed through the press and afterward, when the stamp was completed, it could be unfolded, showing broken fragments of printing in different places on an irregularly shaped piece of paper. These varieties were uncommon, and they belong in the error and rarity class of stamp collecting.

Another premium stamp in coils is the line-pair. Naturally, to have a line stamp you must have two joined together with their perforations. Every so often a line runs between two of the stamps in a coil strip. This line is a guide line for use in the printing process. Since line-pairs are far less frequent in the roll than ordinary pairs, occurring about every twenty-fifth stamp, the price is higher—sometimes quite considerably higher—than the normal pair.

For that matter, coil stamps are usually higher than their regular counterparts. Perhaps one reason for this is that fewer coil stamps are purchased at post offices by collectors, most of them being sold

A coil line-pair and a regular pair of coil stamps for comparison. Line-pairs occur about every twenty-fifth stamp in the coil.

to companies with large mailing lists. This is because of the large quantity of stamps in a coil—100, 300, or 500. While a postal clerk will break a sheet of stamps to sell the customer one single stamp, he will not break a coil. One must purchase the entire quantity, which, especially in the larger denominations, can run into a respectable cost.

Also, coil stamps are often made in two styles—perforated horizontally, with the stamps printed sideways on the strip; or perforated vertically, the stamp impressions being right side up on the strip. This is because coil stamps are used in affixing and vending machines, which, in turn, are made by different companies and handle the stamps differently.

Early coil stamps were sold in imperforate rolls, to be perforated by the machine as they were dispensed. These machines sold stamps to the public the same way stamp machines work today, except that the stamps were chopped from the coil as they were ejected, with many different kinds of perforations. Some of the ways these stamps were separated was by cutting large rectangular holes between the stamps, the remaining paper being sheared as the stamp was taken from the machine. In the vending machines in use today, regularly perforated coils are inserted, the machine cutting off the required number right through the perforations. This spoils the coil stamp for collections, since much of the

This early coil stamp shows the private perforation of the Schermack Mailing Machine Company of Detroit, Michigan.

perforations are lost by the knife. Unless the machine vends four coil stamps at one time, so the center pair can be separated by tearing the perforations normally (the outer two stamps used for postage), it is best not to buy coil stamps from machines for a collection, but to pay the premium price to a dealer in order to get undamaged specimens.

Chapter Six

Semipostal Stamps

Foreign countries often issue stamps in manners which the United States has never used. Semipostal stamps, for example, are issued by a great many countries, especially those in middle Europe. There are two values on such stamps, and the stamps are sold for the combined amounts.

The regular postage value is the only amount the stamp is authorized to use as postage. The second amount is turned over to various government agencies for different uses. Switzerland issues annual sets of semipostal stamps captioned PRO JUVEN-TUTE. Translated, this means "for children," and the surplus value on each stamp is used for child welfare. Issues are also printed for PRO PATRIA and

This set of semipostal stamps was issued to help the finances of the Antwerp Zoo.

the proceeds devoted to helping various national institutions such as museums and libraries, as well as poor people.

The Netherlands issues stamps titled WINTER-HULP, and these are devoted to winter aid for the destitute.

Almost any charity can benefit from the issuance of semipostal stamps, whichever one is designated to receive the surplus value of the stamps. It seems an easy way to tax the populace for whatever needs arise. Semipostals were issued both as postage stamps and as souvenir sheets, some of which command astronomical prices today.

Belgium has issued a great number of semipostal stamps devoted to the restoration of many abbeys and churches destroyed during the wars. Orval Abbey alone is responsible for several large issues of stamps, and the revenue derived from their sale has restored the great religious relic.

Of course, issuing semipostal stamps makes the post office perform the duty of acting as the financial department of the charities involved. In Europe this is not too far out of line with the regular duties of the post office. In the British Empire the post office handles the telephone facilites and other civil services, so the collection of the semipostal tax is well within the scope of the department. However, Great Britain does not issue semipostals.

Chapter Seven

Packets and Mixtures

For the person just beginning to collect stamps, perhaps the best way to start is to purchase mixtures and packets. Mixtures are sold—presumably "as is" and often labeled "unsorted." However, you may depend upon the mixture having been looked over for removal of any stamps worth more than a couple of cents, leaving the common stamps only.

This need not deter you from acquiring a mixture or two, though, since even the common stamps are of value in a collection and very necessary to fill in the countries as you go. As a matter of fact, the great majority of stamps from every country are cheap and "common," only the higher values or the rarities being of greater worth.

Bag mixtures like this can be bought in dime stores and department and toy stores.

Topical packets come on many different subjects. These stamps are all different, and most of them are used. Some are canceled to order.

Mixtures are gathered in several different manners. Bank mixtures and Mission mixtures presumably are collected from the postage sent to banks and missions throughout the world. The stamps on incoming mail are torn off with a small piece of the envelope, and these packed in bags sold by weight.

The idea is that the stamps are unsorted, and you will thereby stand a good chance of finding several specimens of good value. Be this as it may, the mixtures are a good way to get a world-wide collection started.

You will usually find many duplicates of each stamp in such a mixture, but you will also end up with several hundred different stamps from all over the world. Then you can begin to fill in the different sets as you go along completing a country. Sometimes mixtures are offered "off paper." This means that the stamps have been soaked off the envelopes, so you pay only for the stamps and not for the corners of the envelopes. The price of such mixtures is higher than on-paper mixtures, and the off-paper ones are not usually sold by weight, but rather by count—100 stamps, 200, 500, 1,000, 5,000, etc.

Some of the dealers advertise that their mixtures are of a given number "all different." This means that the stamps have been sorted into sets or individual specimens, and that there are no duplicates in the accumulation. Naturally, the prices of these stamps is higher than that of mixtures containing duplicates.

Another way of buying mixtures is by individual countries. You will see ads listing 1,000 different stamps from Italy, for example, or 250 different stamps from Iceland. This is an excellent way to begin collecting any given country. But if your interest is in building up a collection of world-wide stamps, then such a mixture from each country will give you many of the lesser values to fill in spaces, and you can go on from there buying individual stamps to complete issues.

When stamps are sold as individual country items, they are usually called packets, rather than mixtures. Packets are made up for sale containing from 2 to 10,000 stamps and even more.

Often dealers will offer a packet of stamps free when you ask for their stamp approvals. This means that you will, in fact, receive the packet as advertised, and you will also receive stamps on approval. More about approval stamps in a later chapter. Here, I just wish to advise that in sending for approvals, you send only to large, well-established, well-known dealers. You will have a lot less grief if you do.

Another way of buying stamps in packets is by years. Ads will read, for example, Canada, 1968 (12) $1.60; 1969 (4) $.38; 1970 (11) $2.10; 1971 (22) $3.15. These code figures mean that the stamps of Canada are being offered by each year. All the stamps issued by that country in that particular year are in each packet. As listed above —and the figures are arbitrarily taken out of the air for purposes of illustrating the idea—in 1968 Canada published 12 stamps (the number in paren-

Packets are sold by individual countries. Usually "short" sets lacking the high values. The set illustrated was canceled to order, not actually used as postage.

theses), which the dealer is selling for $1.60 complete. In 1969 the country issued 4 stamps, and in 1971, 22 stamps. Again, these are not factual numbers but just for illustration.

One thing about mixtures that makes them of greater interest than buying stamps singly is the fact that the stamps included in the mixtures have actually seen postal duty. In recent years the demand for used stamps of foreign countries has led dealers and postal departments of some countries to "cancel to order" stamps from their localities. This,

In a mixture envelope like this, at least you are sure that the cancellations are genuine, and that the stamps have seen postal duty as intended.

to me, is not a good practice, and in my own mind, makes the stamp little better than a counterfeit. While it is true that such stamps are accepted as genuine specimens in a collection, most catalogues have notes stating that the listed prices are for canceled-to-order stamps, and those specimens having seen actual postal duty are higher. This, in itself, is enough to show that the canceling-to-order practice is not such a good idea.

A packet and Mini-Album are sold by the post offices and contain one each of every stamp issued during the year.

In any event, you must determine whether or not you wish to collect used or mint stamps or mixed. If used stamps do not appeal to your taste, then all this discussion about mixtures and packets is lost, since they contain *only* used stamps, and you must look elsewhere for the mint varieties.

Mint stamps are sold in packets as well as used stamps. You simply must look for the designation as to whether or not the items offered are mint. Mint stamps are sold in sets—usually two ways. A "short" set, contains all the lower values, and a complete set contains all the values of any particular issue.

Our government has gone into the packet-selling business in a way, by issuing what are called Mini-Albums. These are issued by the year, and each album, which is a cardboard folder, contains a packet of mint stamps—every stamp issued during that year. The folder contains printed information concerning the stamps, a glassine envelope of stamp hinges, and a card telling you how to mount the stamps in the Mini-Album. The one for the year 1971 is now on sale at post offices for $2.50 per copy.

Time was when stamp dealers sold stamps as individual items, and it was a very great part of the thrill and interest in collecting stamps to sit at a dealer's counter, an opened album in front of you—or perhaps a stock book—filled with all the stamps in the dealer's stock. Hours could be spent poring over each item before you made your choice, finally taking only those specimens you wanted, paying for them as single items. Today, the trend is to sell stamps in issue sets, already separated and placed in glassine envelopes. You don't even see the individual stamps until you get them home and take them out of the envelope. A lot of the thrill of collecting is lost in this method of buying.

Fortunately some dealers still let you look through their albums or stock books, selecting your purchase according to your wants or needs. Patronize these dealers as much as possible to continue that wonderful method of stamp collecting.

The sets, put up in glassine envelopes, are usually "short" sets of the lower values of any given issue. It is a good practice, when the sets are first issued by the countries, to purchase the entire issue. The short sets are usually sold for a few cents over face value, and the higher values sold as single items at some fraction of catalogue value. If you stop at the short set, there is a good chance that as soon as the stamp issue has been sold out, the higher values will jump in price to the point where it is difficult to purchase them.

It is very frustrating to see a new issue come out to sell for, say, $2.50 for the complete set of all values, but you only bought the short lower values for 69 cents. Then, a few months later, when you do decide to fill in the issue, you find that the higher values of that set are now selling for $10 or $12. Of course, the great majority of stamps do not increase in value so drastically, and I am only using arbitrary figures to illustrate my point, but the idea is there, and there is an excellent possibility of stamps doing just that. This is particularly true in those countries which are in constant and high demand. These include the stamps of the United Nations, Israel, Vatican City, and a few other countries. Stamps of these countries should be purchased as soon after they have been issued as you can obtain them in order to insure your getting them at fairly reasonable prices. Also, the stamps of such countries are good investment items as a general rule. Their value increases steadily and fairly rapidly, and there is always the possibility of selling them at a profit either to a dealer or to a collector who missed the issues.

Stamps from such countries are sometimes sold in packets, but almost never are they to be found in mixtures.

Chapter Eight

———————

Souvenir Sheets and Cards

A great many countries have issued a great many stamps in specially prepared sheets. These are called souvenir sheets, and usually are issued to commemorate some event, person, political happening, or almost anything. Sometimes—most times, in fact—the sheet consists of one stamp, usually a replica of a stamp already issued as regular postage, on a sheet with wide margins all around, bearing the inscriptions for the issuance of the souvenir. This is to say, a commemorative stamp may be issued to commemorate, for example, the birthday of a national figure, and simultaneously a souvenir sheet bearing the imprint of the same stamps is issued.

Most of the time the value of the souvenir sheet

A stamp like this would be an item in either a souvenir sheet collection or in a music topical collection.

rises higher than that of the stamp, although this is not necessarily so. A large number of souvenir sheets do not increase enough in value to make it worthwhile to collect them as an investment, but some of them shoot up sky high. Such was the case with the souvenir sheet of the United States commemorating the battle of White Plains. This sheet of twenty-five 2-cent stamps selling when issued for 50 cents, now is catalogued at $175.

This Polish souvenir sheet is rapidly rising in value. It was issued to commemorate a stratospheric balloon flight.

Often a pair of sheets are issued—one perforated and the other imperforate. European countries do this more often than the United States. This necessitates the purchase of both sheets to have the issue complete. The last souvenir sheet issued by this country was in 1966, depicting the not very pretty stamps issued for the Sixth International Philatelic Exhibition. For that matter, the year 1966 was a year of particularly uninteresting and ugly stamps

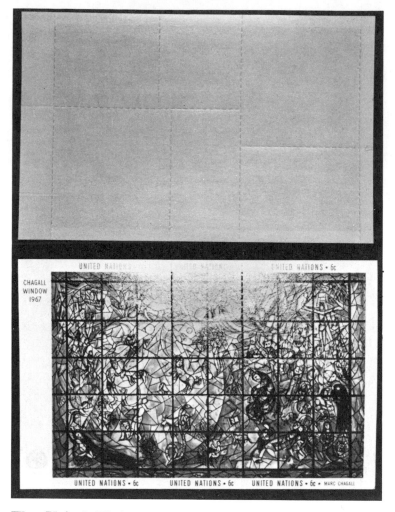

The United Nations souvenir sheet is actually six 6-cent stamps rouletted so they can be separated to use individually as postage.

for this country, the one exception being the stamp issued for the Beautification of America, which, by the way, was designed by a Japanese girl, Miss Gyo Fujikawa.

Sometimes the stamp or stamps on a souvenir sheet are the same size, denomination, and color as the stamp of the regular commemorative issue. And if the sheet is perforated, the stamp may be torn out and then be impossible to distinguish from the regular stamp. Often the stamp on the sheet is printed in a different color, or the size may be changed, in which case, of course, if the stamp is removed from the sheet it is still distinguishable from the regular issue.

An interesting souvenir sheet was issued by the New York City office of the United Nations in 1967. It portrays a stained-glass window made by Marc Chagall, and the sheet is printed in the somber blues of the original window. What makes this sheet unique is that it is in reality, six 6-cent stamps, the sheet being rouletted in order to permit separation into the individual stamps. Each stamp is a different size and shape, and each stamp, when torn from the sheet, shows one detail of the window.

Souvenir cards are issued for sale at certain philatelic or civic affairs. For example, cards have been issued to commemorate the major philatelic exhibitions, and other gatherings of postal significance. Such cards were issued for the 14th International Stamp Exhibition held in New York City on March 17, 1972. This exhibition immediately became known by a compound word composed of the abbreviations of the title—Interpex—as were all the other exhibitions; Cipex, Tipex, etc.

The card issued for this particular exhibition shows a block of four of the 4-cent Communications for Peace stamp, issued in 1960, and carries an inscription, vignetted in the background of which are three other stamps pertaining to space. The collecting of souvenir cards has jumped tremendously in the past few years, and now the prices of some of them are rising abnormally. Usually the purchase of these cards is limited to four or five to a person at the exhibitions, which policy immediately causes a rush to get more if possible by having friends purchase them or by going several times to the counter to buy the quota. Anything that causes a demand for an item of philately is bound also to cause a price rise, and this makes souvenir cards a fairly good investment item.

Three new cards have been printed recently. They commemorate the inauguration of the new United States Postal Service in July 1971; the Inter-American Philatelic Exposition, held in Rio de Janeiro, Brazil, in August 1972; and the combined summer and winter Olympic games, held in Sapporo, Japan, and Munich, East Germany, also issued in August 1972. These last cards are inscribed in German and were sold at the Munich games. One each of the four United States Olympic stamps are depicted on the cards, which were sold for $1.00 each. I suppose the card will be called Olphex, or some similar combination.

This souvenir card, the second to be devoted to United States' accomplishments in space, depicts the vignette from the Echo 1 Commemorative postage stamp of 1960. That issue hailed the achievement of a significant advancement toward world peace through closer communication and wider exchange of viewpoints.

The background tint of the card comprises enlargements of four other postage stamps which depicted space-related subjects: the 1948 Commemorative honoring the Centennial Anniversary of Fort Bliss, the initial Army center for rocket and guided missile research and development; the Air Mail Commemorative honoring Robert H. Goddard, modern rocketry pioneer, issued in 1964; and the twin 8¢ Decade of Space Achievement Commemorative of 1971.

INTERPEX NEW YORK, N.Y.
14TH INTERNATIONAL STAMP EXHIBITION
MARCH 17–19, 1972

Some of these souvenir cards cost hundreds of dollars. And they aren't all that old.

The main difference between souvenir sheets and souvenir cards is that the sheets are, in actuality, a postal item and as such can be used as postage for regular or air mail. The cards, on the other hand, are items of postal significance, but they cannot be used postally—nor can the stamps shown on them be cut apart to be used for postage. They fall into the category of items of philatelic interest, some persons ignoring stamps altogether in favor of specimens like these.

Chapter Nine

Errors and Rarities

For almost every stamp collector who learns something about stamps, the great ambition is to find an error or come across some rare stamps. Except in the case of a near miracle (finding an error in the post office), such items must be purchased from other stamp collectors or from dealers. The prices are high.

With old rare stamps, any pieces should be left in the condition they are found. A "piece" is the term given to more than one stamp still held together by the perforations or, in the case of an imperforate stamp, by the margin between. In other words, if you have a strip of two or three, or an irregular block of any number of specimens, do not

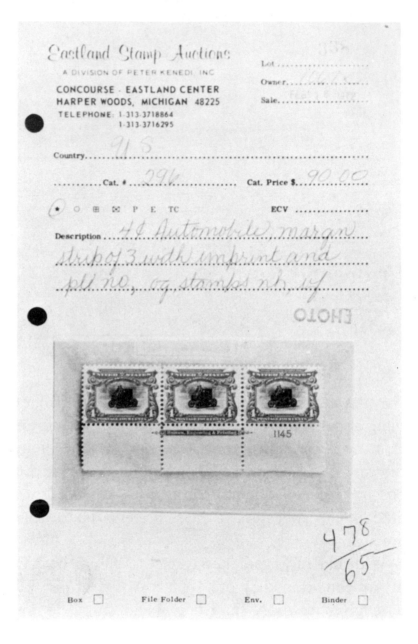

Eastland Stamp Auctions

A DIVISION OF PETER KENEDI, INC

CONCOURSE · EASTLAND CENTER
HARPER WOODS, MICHIGAN 48225
TELEPHONE: 1-313-3718864
 1-313-3716295

Lot ....

Owner ....

Sale ....

Country ...... 𝓤 𝓢 ....

.... Cat. # ... 296 .... Cat. Price $ ... 90.00 ...

(*) O ⊞ ⊠ P E TC   ECV ....

Description ...... 4¢ Automobile margin
strip of 3 with imprint and
plt no., og, stamps nh, if

PHOTO

1145

478/65

Box ☐   File Folder ☐   Env. ☐   Binder ☐

This is the way stamps are received from one auction dealer. The inverted rubber stamped "photo" means that the item was illustrated in the dealer's catalogue.

separate them but leave them intact. A piece, especially if the stamp has some value, always has a higher value than the same number of single stamps.

While it is true that so many people have been made conscious of the value of old postage stamps in the past half-century, and the chance of finding rarities is greatly reduced, still there must be many, many items worth a small fortune to stamp collectors, lying in musty attics or down in basements, stored in old trunks, boxes, and bales.

Whenever access is available to an old attic or storage room, be sure to look over every paper very carefully in search of stamps on envelopes, cards, on old stock certificates, or any other legal document. Some revenue stamps are of considerable

This old carrier envelope found in an attic is interesting but not of too much value. (Cover courtesy Cynthia Lowry, West Shokan, New York.)

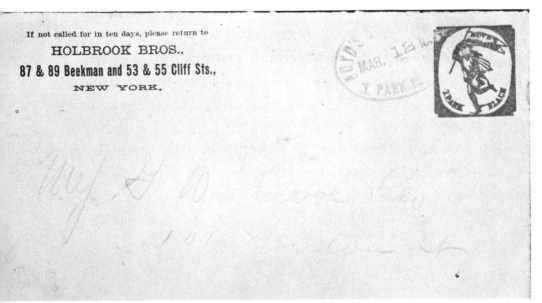

value too, you know. Often pieces of old stamps are found in an old discarded and stored away box or jewel box. These were left over from the postage used by the long-dead person. Perhaps they wrote many letters and bought stamps in sheets or parts of sheets, then when they died what stamps were left were forgotten and stored with other personal effects. Some of these old stamps could be worth a fortune, because they would be in mint condition. So don't neglect to look for such treasures whenever you have the chance. Not all the good stamps have been discovered.

While on the average an error rises greatly in value, sometimes a genuine error in a stamp can be bought for a very low price. This usually comes about when the error was made so often, or so many of the errors were printed that the supply is enough to meet the demand. Sometimes the demand is so small that the poor stamp goes begging for want of collectors to treasure it, and this in turn would tend to keep the price down. Such is the case with the two German errors illustrated here. They only cost a few dollars each, instead of several hundred or several thousand dollars each. Why they are not more valuable I cannot definitely say, but it is safe to say that the supply is great enough to more than meet the demand, and the stamps were not very popular in the first place.

Not so with the famous Graf Zeppelin issue of

The well-known error on the 3-pfennig German Stamp was made in such quantity that it still can be bought for a few dollars. The regular stamp is also shown.

this country. These air mail stamps were issued to commemorate the first round-trip flight of that enormous flying sausage from Europe to Pan America. The face value of the set of three stamps was $4.55, and I can well remember when they went on sale in the post offices. I did not buy any because of the odd values. I didn't think they were worth the price. Evidently almost everyone else thought much the same way, because of the more than one million stamps of each value that were printed, less than 10 per cent were sold— only slightly over 5 per cent of the two higher values. Finally the issue was withdrawn, and over 90 per cent of the stamps were destroyed. Today the catalogue value is over $600 for a set of *single stamps!* So much for my sound judgment!

There are many very unhappy stamp collectors around who had the chance to buy these in the post office but didn't—the author being one of them.

Another German error so common that it never went high in value. This shows an inverted surcharge on an already surcharged stamp.

Not all stamps rise so dramatically in value, and it is nearly impossible to judge which ones will. Of course, going back to the amount of money you have to lay out for your hobby, the answer is to buy everything that is issued, save them and watch to see which ones go up. If, within a few years, they still remain fairly cheap, then it is safe to assume they are not ever going to do anything, and you can dump them.

When collecting rarities, errors, or valuable varieties of stamps, whether or not they are mint, foreign or of this country, you should be as selective and as picky as you possibly can be. The reason most people collect these items is because of their value, and because they expect them to go still higher in value before they are disposed of at a profit.

Such things as a missing perforation will reduce the value of an otherwise good stamp when you sell it. This is especially true of corner perforations. There may be a crease in the paper of the stamp, so small as to go unnoticed unless you examine it closely or use a glass. Be certain, if the stamp is of any great value, that the buyer *will* use a glass, and the crease will *not* pass unnoticed. If the perforations are very uneven, it will lower the price. If the colored design of the stamp is unevenly centered within the perforations, that is another point against the ultimate selling value. A stamp, normally perforated, having one edge without perforations, is of less value than a perfect copy. These stamps are called straight-edged stamps. Avoid them if at all possible.

Mint stamps without gum are of less value than regular gummed specimens. Usually such a stamp was glued to an album page or in a stock book by humidity. Or it may have become stuck to other stamps, making it necessary to soak them apart, thus losing the gum. Make no attempt to regum a stamp to restore it to good condition. First, you cannot duplicate the gum used by the government. Secondly, you cannot spread it evenly on the stamp. Thirdly, you cannot know the exact thickness to apply the gum. If you lose the gum on a mint

Pairs of the Defense issue of 1940, imperforate between, are worth much more than the ordinary perforated stamps.

stamp, you should just try to accept your loss as philosophically as possible.

The same with parted perforations in blocks of stamps. If you have a block on which some of the perforations have parted, you merely have four stamps. No longer can you value it at the premium price of a block. The best thing to do is to part the stamps, saving an intact pair if possible, and make two separate singles.

The ultimate aim and desire of every ardent stamp collector is to obtain a specimen of every stamp printed in whatever category he is collecting. If he collects general world stamps, his aim is impossible from the very start, since there are several stamps of which only one single copy is known to exist. Such an example is the crude, ugly, miserably colored stamp—the 1-penny magenta British Guiana. This unsightly piece of paper, colored a bilious purplish-reddish-bluish, recently sold for the not inconsiderable sum of—hold on to the book—$280,000! Dear reader, that horrible example of postage is the most beautiful stamp in the world!

The United States air mail stamp, 24-cent face value issued in 1918, with the center inverted, goes for about $35,000 per stamp now. So you see, not even President Roosevelt, who had a lot of money and who was one of the world's greatest philatelists, could achieve his ultimate goal of possessing a specimen of every stamp issued.

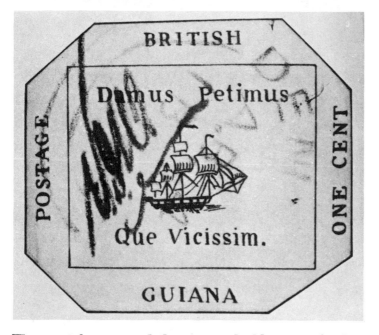

The most famous and the most valuable stamp in the world today. Only one copy is known to exist. It recently sold for a quarter of a million dollars.

So you compromise. You can collect rarities and errors as far as your finances allow, but do not let the fact that completion is impossible deter you from the great enjoyment found in lesser copies.

Varieties in stamps are many. Some of them become quite valuable. These varieties may range from color differences, shades of colors, perforation differences, to whether the stamp was printed on a flat-bed press or a rotary press. There are also plate differences—those caused by damage or wear on a plate causing a slight change to be made. The change was usually not deliberate, but was the result of two different engravers working on the same plate. If a nick was suffered on a plate, for example, an engraver—other than the one who originally did the plate—might have been assigned to repair it. The slight differences that showed up in the subsequent printing of that stamp made it a collectable variety—sometimes a highly priced rarity.

Sometimes a printing plate will crack, and several sheets of stamps run off and issued before the crack is noticed. These are immediately in great demand

This little stamp with the airplane flying upside down will cost you $35,000 if you want to add it to your collection.

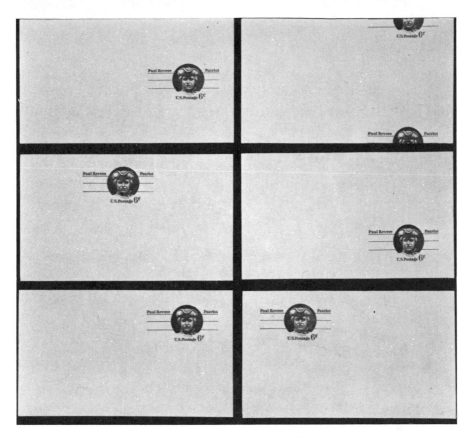

A regular postal card and five "cutting" errors of the same card—worth exactly nothing because they were made by the author to illustrate the fakes possible.

among variety collectors since the supply is limited. As soon as the crack is detected the plate is either withdrawn or repaired.

Varieties also exist in the kind of paper used to print the stamps. Sometimes the paper was thick, sometimes thin. Some papers were soft and porous; others hard and non-porous. All these things contribute to the creation of varieties which are the delight of specializing collectors, and sometimes the bane of those general collectors who do not recognize the interest or additional value in the differences.

In recent years a new category has sprung up in the stamp-collecting field, called EFOs. This means Errors, Freaks, and Oddities. Actually, the error part of this title does not include the real error rarities—such as inverted centers and similar mistakes—but minor errors are included.

Many of the items listed as freaks are off-center perforations—where the perforation is so far off center as to cut right through the center of the stamp or, in many cases, cut off one portion of the stamp, placing that portion of the stamp above or below it, or perhaps to the side. Sometimes, in multiple-color printings, one color is shifted to a degree that it makes a strange design on the stamp instead of the intended impression. These are given names to classify them, such as, the "kicking rifle," on a stamp bearing the printing of a kneeling rifleman with the stamp so off center that the man and his gun are at the extreme right end of the stamp. The idea being that the recoil of the gun knocked the man across the stamp. This is, to me, so fanciful an idea as to be ridiculous, but nevertheless it happened.

Sometimes the perforations are so far off center that the name or the value of the stamp—normally, say, on the bottom—is cut off entirely from its proper location and appears instead at the top of the stamp below. This means, of course, that all the stamps in that sheet will be the same, except the first row which will be lacking the name or value entirely, having a wide margin instead. It would appear that this row would be of greater value than all the other stamps, since in a normal sheet of United States commemoratives, for example, there would be only ten of the nameless or valueless stamps to the remaining forty with the displaced name or value. Never having collected these kinds of stamps, I cannot definitely say that this is so but it seems logical.

I can readily see that these kinds of rarities would be fun to collect, and that they would have a value over the regular stamp of that issue. The only thing I take exception to is the outlandish names given to the specimens to describe them.

Color variation is another category that is in great favor among specializing collectors. These people will make a collection of dozens, or even hundreds of specimens of the same stamp, separating them into infinite minute shades of color. Another way of collecting is position collecting. This is done more with the stamps of Great Britain than with other countries, since the older British stamps had a letter or symbol in one or more corners of each stamp, designating its position in the printed sheet. The idea behind position collecting is to obtain every stamp in a sheet, mounting them in the original positions they occupied until an entire sheet is reconstructed.

A word or two about counterfeit errors should be given here. Often you will find someone offering for sale a post card "error." The stamps may be in the lower left-hand corner instead of its regular position in the upper right. Or the card may have half the stamp in the upper right corner and the other half in the lower right corner. Any number of "errors" in the cards may be suggested.

Actually, these are fakes, and they have no value as errors at all. The fact is, it is possible to purchase post cards from some of the large post offices in uncut sheets of forty cards. You may cut these sheets up in any way you wish, to create "errors" and many unscrupulous persons have been able to palm off such "errors" at enormous prices to unwary individuals. They need not necessarily be beginners, only persons unfamiliar with the way post cards are made and sold in the post offices.

The way to deal with these persons if you are ever offered such a rarity as a post card "error" is very simple. Merely say that you would be happy to purchase the error as an investment, if they will have it authenticated by the Scott Stamp and Coin Company, H. E. Harris, Minkus, or any other of the leading stamp dealers in the world, and present it to you with the certificate of authentication. You

can even offer to pay the cost of the authentication
—after he has the certificate—*not* in advance. I
think you will find your salesman making a hasty
exit, taking his "treasures" with him.

Counterfeiting is big business, especially in
stamps of countries that are no longer in existence,
and whose legal stamps are very high-priced. Many
of the old European states issuing their own postage
actually had very little traffic in postal duty. Their
stamps are worth a couple of dollars unused, but
several hundred, perhaps, if canceled. Hence, counterfeit cancellations are very plentiful. If you buy
such stamps, it is best to buy from a large dealer
who will authenticate the stamp and the cancellation, and issue a guarantee certificate attesting to
its genuineness. You will pay for this service, naturally, but the alternative is the possibility of ending
up with a worthless piece of ornamental paper.

And then, of course, there are the out-and-out
counterfeits. Almost every valuable stamp of the
world has been counterfeited at one time or another.
Some of the rarer items are so plentiful as counterfeits that it is nearly impossible to find a genuine
copy. Of course, the fact that it was nearly impossible to find a genuine copy in the first place is what
made the stamp valuable to begin with.

It would seem very easy to counterfeit some of
the older rarities, since they were so crudely made
by their governments. They were wood-block prints

The sheet of forty postal cards is almost as big as the pretty model holding it. You can buy them at large post offices at face value.

This set of stamps is counterfeit. You must be very careful when buying old and rare stamps because many counterfeits exist.

If genuine, this Austrian stamp would be worth about $500. The stamp *is* genuine—the *cancellation* is a forgery! Unused, the stamp is worth 50 cents.

on soft, spongy paper, the dyes imperfect and im-
perfectly applied to the printing die. The impressions were often off-center and sometimes almost
illegible. All these things make it easier for the
counterfeiter, and for this reason you should be very
sure, when you buy such a rarity, that you know for
certain that the stamp is genuine. Authentication
by a reputable and knowledgeable dealer is the best
way.

Chapter Ten

Stamps Other Than Postage

Almost every country issues stamps for other than postal duty and for use only within the limits of that country. These take the form of revenue stamps, tax stamps, hunting permit stamps (such as our own "duck" stamps), postage-due stamps, and many more varieties.

Revenue stamps are issued in great numbers in the United States, and the collection of revenue stamps can become a very difficult hobby. This is so because of the number that have been issued, and the variety of the issues, as well as the difficulty in obtaining a copy of each kind.

Revenue stamps are issued by the Department of Internal Revenue and are affixed to almost every-

A group of different Internal Revenue stamps, one with an inverted overprint.

thing—commodities as well as documents, legal papers, all kinds of tobacco products, narcotics, perfumes, wines and liquors. In fact, almost everything is subject to the affixation of a revenue stamp. Even potatoes have their revenue stamps!

Two sets of revenue stamps, one with an overprint of value the same as the face value of the stamp.

The Department of Internal Revenue has issued stamps with face values of many thousands of dollars—even $10,000 stamps are available. This does not necessarily mean that the stamps cost $10,000, but that it is for use on some product or document, such as a stock certificate, having that value. These very high face-value revenue stamps sell for a few dollars each, canceled, and sometimes for only a very little more than that, mint. They signify that that amount of tax was paid.

Most of the revenue stamps are canceled with a heavy obliterating mark, but often punch cancellations are used. The individual firms using the stamps use a punch with a patterned perforating device—perhaps the name of the company—which is applied to the stamp and the document it is affixed to. The holes punched through both the stamp and the paper effectively "tied" the stamp to the document, making it impossible to fake anything about the transaction. Stamps with such punched cancellations usually have less value than stamps canceled with inking devices.

Revenue stamps are found on many things in daily use. For instance, if you purchase a deck of cards, the wrapper will be sealed with a playing-card revenue stamp. Every pack of cigarettes has a revenue stamp sealing it. Cigar boxes are closed with such a stamp. Perfume bottles often have a sealing revenue stamp affixed in such a way that it must be torn when the bottle is opened. These stamps attest to the fact that the manufacturer paid the revenue or taxes due on his product.

Another example of revenue stamp was the old automobile use stamps. These were the forerunners

A cut cancellation. Stamps punched like this have less value than specimens canceled with ink.

Three different kinds of playing-card revenue stamps. You may have seen one on a deck of cards.

The old auto-use stamps had the gum on the face, as shown by the reflections on the middle stamp. The back was filled out with pertinent information about the car.

of our present inspection stickers and were issued from 1942 until 1946. You had to have one stuck on the windshield of your car in order to operate the vehicle. The gum was on the face of the stamp, and the back had several lines to be filled out with the make, serial number, etc. pertaining to the car. The values started with $5.00, sold for affixing to the car in July, then dropping in increments of approximately 42 cents for each month of the year, running from July to July. That is, if you registered your car in July you would have to pay $5.00 for the stamp. If you registered the vehicle in May, for example, the stamp would have a face value of only 84 cents because you would have been paying only the fee for the remaining two months of the automobile registration year.

In 1960 the government began issuing boating stamps, required for every boat over ten horsepower. These have a face value of $3.00 and $1.00. They are issued by the United States Coast Guard and are obtained through your post office.

In 1907 the United States issued International Reply Coupons to be sold at the post offices to prepay the reply letter from a foreign country. All members of the Universal Postal Union issued such coupons. If you wrote, for example, to Germany and wanted to enclose a self-addressed, stamped envelope, this would naturally be impossible. The envelope would be no problem, but the stamp

A War Savings stamp. They came in several denominations and were sold in post offices.

would. So you purchased an International Reply Coupon at the post office and sent that along with your letter. The person you wrote to, in turn, took the coupon to his post office, which exchanged the coupon for enough postage to answer your letter. You paid the equivalent here in United States currency. Kind of handy.

During World War I, in 1917 to be exact, the United States printed War Savings stamps. The first ones were called Thrift Stamps. In 1918 they were changed to War Savings Certificate stamps, having a face value of $5.00. The stamps were purchased in 1918 at the post office for $4.12 in January, the cost increasing by 1 cent per month until in December, the stamp would cost you $4.23. Then you kept the stamp for five years, redeeming it at the post office for $5.00 in 1923. War Savings stamps were also sold during World War II.

In 1954, the government issued Postal Savings stamps in the denominations of 10 cents, 25 cents, 50 cents, $1.00, and $5.00. These stamps were pasted into little books, which, when filled with the proper amount, were exchanged for United States Savings Bonds. The stamps were discontinued in 1970.

In 1934 the United States began to print a series of stamps issued for the purpose of collecting funds for establishing refuges for migratory waterfowl. These are commonly called duck stamps, since they are primarily issued as a license to hunt ducks, geese, and other waterfowl.

The first issues had a face value of $1.00 and they were sold at post offices throughout the country. The first issue sold well under one million copies. The last issue sold well over three million copies, and the price has increased from $1.00 to $3.00. There is a rumor that next year the price may jump to $5.00.

These duck stamps were designed to be pasted to the purchaser's hunting license and signed in ink over the face of the stamp to validate it as a hunting permit. They are in great demand among specializing collectors, and some of them are worth much more than their face values.

Most of the duck stamps are beautiful works of art. Designs are submitted each year to the government from many artists on a competitive basis. No

Duck stamps had this warning printed on the back. The stamps were supposed to be stuck on your hunting permit.

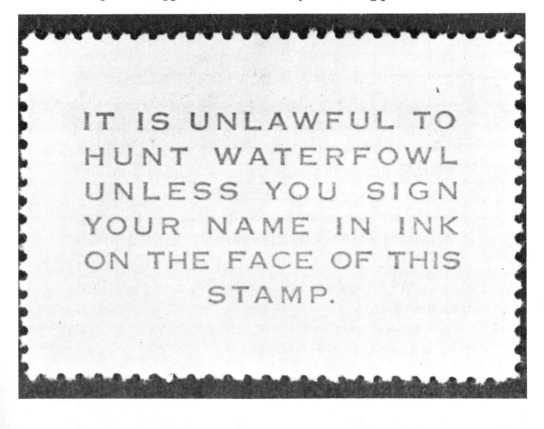

payment is made to the artist winning the competition, other than the recognition given him for being the designer of that particular stamp and a special album containing a full sheet of the stamps.

Certain restrictions are placed on the competition. Each design submitted must contain one or more waterfowl, of a species not previously used on any other duck stamp. The painting may be in water color, oils, pastels, or any other medium the artist prefers. Maynard Reece is the artist who has won more of the contests than any other artist. His winning designs appear on the stamps of 1948, 1951, 1959, 1969, and 1971.

The first, second, third, fourth, fifth, eighth, and ninth duck stamps are the ones having the highest increase in value at the time of this writing. There is an error recorded for the first issue only, as imperforate, listing at $750 per specimen, and as imperforate horizontally, which would have to be collected as a pair in order to show the error.

The only stamp of the series to show anything other than waterfowl to date is the 1959 issue, which depicts a labrador retriever holding a mallard drake in its mouth. The stamp bears the inscription, "retrievers save game," and the idea was that since waterfowl were becoming scarce at that time, hunting should be done with dogs trained to hunt for, find, and bring back to their owners, any game birds shot and lost.

Duck stamps are void after the year they are issued as hunting permits, and each stamp bears the inscription "void after —" (whatever year the stamp is issued in). Postage stamps of the United States, of course, are not voided.

Another kind of revenue stamp was printed on documents, such as the check shown in the illustration. This is called revenue paper, and while the imprint is indeed a revenue stamp, it is not used for anything other than the tax on the checks drawn with the imprint on them. Some collectors specialize in collecting these kinds of items.

Telegraph stamps are another variety of stamp that was issued for a specific purpose other than actual postal duty. These stamps were issued by private companies for use on their telegrams and were first issued by the American Rapid Telegraph Company in 1881. In 1894 this company became a part of the great Western Union Telegraph Com-

Revenue paper like this old check is uncommon, but not especially valuable.

pany. Telegraph stamps were discontinued after 1946.

In the year 1907 the first Christmas Seals were issued in the country, by the Delaware Chapter of the American Red Cross. The money raised from the sales of seals was for use by charities. Today, Christmas Seals are issued for the relief of tuberculosis. From the humble beginning of about $4,000 in sales in 1907, Christmas Seals now gross nearly 35 million dollars per year. While most of the seals may be purchased for a few cents each from stamp dealers, some of the earlier issues have a much greater value, running as high as $100 for a perfect specimen. Collecting these seals is considered a branch of philately because of the use of Christmas Seals on letters.

Telegraph stamps like these from the Western Union Company are no longer used on telegrams.

Chapter Eleven

Customer Deposit Accounts

In the past few years the United States has adopted a system of selling stamps and other philatelic items directly from the source, on what are called Customer Deposit Accounts. Many governments throughout the world have long used this method of boosting their philatelic sales.

Any person wishing to subscribe to the service sends in an amount of money to the agency, placing the amount on deposit. Then, as the items are issued, they are mailed automatically, insuring that the subscriber gets the items even though he or she is not aware of their publication.

So far, the importance of this method is in the purchase of souvenir pages, post office poster bulletins, and special items. It may include the sales of stamp issues in the near future.

As of June 1972 the subscription had to be opened with the minimum amount of $10. The first items sold were the souvenir pages of the 1972 National Parks issue. When the supply of these pages is exhausted, presumably the sales will stop. The United States Government has, however, been known to reissue popular-selling items, thus dropping the value of the initial issue in the hands of the collectors who went to considerable time and trouble to collect them.

The address to which subscription deposit amounts are to be sent is:

> Philatelic Automatic Distribution Service
> Philatelic Sales Unit
> Washington, D.C. 20036

Persons wishing to make gifts to someone else of such subscriptions may do so, and a gift card will be sent to the recipient in the name of the giver. The department can cancel any subscription on thirty days notice, refunding any unused portion of the subscription amount to the sender. Notification is sent the subscriber when his account needs replenishing, at which time another $10 is deposited with the service.

A letter to the service should bring additional information as to what items are available, or will be available, and other details of the arrangement.

Another service for collectors is the new-issue service. This is available from any of many dealers specializing in supplying new issues of foreign countries. In this case, you do not have to deposit sums of money in advance, but merely subscribe to the service. The dealer notifies you when new issues are in stock and of the cost of the sets, and you purchase them as desired.

The great advantage of this service is that you are made aware of new issues, which otherwise might slip by you unnoticed unless you carefully read every word in some stamp paper such as *Linn's Stamp Weekly*. Even if you subscribe to a paper, new issues may get by your notice and the services offered by the various dealers are therefore of value.

As a branch of a new-issue service, first day cover services are also offered to those collectors specializing in covers. These dealers keep watch for the new-issue dates and cities, and for a nominal sum supply you with the cachets and covers addressed to you.

Chapter Twelve

Investment Collecting

Investment in postage stamps should not really be called collecting since the real meaning of the word collecting is to obtain as many of a thing as you possibly can, and investment buying of stamps is something entirely different. Actually, investment buying is something that only people who have a surplus of cash can do.

Unless you are so financially situated, investment buying is not for you. The best you can do is to buy a few stamps now and then and hope for the best. The real investment buyer follows every item of news in every periodical devoted to stamps. He is up on world trends, politics in particular, since political changes in countries profoundly affect the value of its postage stamps.

This sheet of telegraph stamps from Spain are not only canceled to order but different cities and different dates appear in the cancellations. It is almost worthless.

Usually, in this age of liberation of small countries from domination by larger countries, stamps play an important part in the general economy. Many of the African states that have gained their freedom and established themselves as individual countries have taken to issuing stamps as fast as they can be printed solely for the purpose of raising money to run their newly founded empires.

Usually, too, these countries make their stamps as beautiful as possible to attract the collector who buys the pretty pictures. This trade goes mostly to young collectors and beginners, but they are also collected by experienced collectors who must add them to their collections if they want to keep up with the stamp developments.

Many of these stamps were never intended to perform actual postal duty. Yet millions of collectors collect canceled stamps in preference to mint ones, and millions more collect both. The answer to this demand was, of course, canceled-to-order stamps, in which entire mint sheets of stamps were canceled at post offices in the issuing countries and sold as canceled varieties.

To a certain degree, dealers also recognize this problem since in pricing a canceled stamp they put one value on it, but if you demand the same stamp in a specimen having actually been used as postage, the price immediately jumps higher. Even in the leading stamp catalogues, there are notes stating that the canceled prices are for canceled-to-order stamps, and stamps having done postal duty are higher.

Not that canceled-to-order stamps are valueless. Unfortunately some of them are so high in cost that they present a strain to purchase them.

Investment buying takes two forms. One is the accumulation of stocks of current stamps, usually in full sheets, and in quantities of those sheets. The other is buying rare and costly items, holding them until they rise higher, then selling them at a profit.

The first category is chancy. Take as an example, the stamps issued by the United States for the four-year period from 1967 to 1971. Speaking only of commemorative stamps, we issued sixteen stamps and one souvenir sheet in 1966; fifteen issues in

1967; twenty-six in 1968; twenty-two stamps in 1969; twenty in 1970, and twenty-three varieties in 1971. These issues total one hundred and twenty-three commemorative stamps, not counting any air mails.

Out of these one hundred twenty-three different issues, one, or rather a *se-tenant* pair of stamps—the space walk issued in 1967—has enjoyed an appreciable rise in value. About four others are slowly rising in value, and in a few years, may realize a very handsome profit. This is a pretty small percentage of the total number of stamps issued. And there is really no sure way to tell as the stamps come out which ones are going to be good investment items.

Experience tells us that, in the case of mint United States commemorative stamps, any stamp dealing with space achievements in any form should go up in time. Also, we feel that any stamp issued in *se-tenant* or composite form should also be worth holding for a time to see what it will do. But these are educated guesses at best, and are founded only on hunch feelings, together with watching what such stamps have done to date. There is no guarantee that they will continue to rise in value, or that they will remain highly priced if they do.

The comforting thing about investing in new issues of our stamps is that you can always get back what you paid for them in face value as postage, or sell them as postage to persons using stamps in quantity, so you won't lose your investment money. But, as for making a profit, this is anybody's guess. For example, I personally believe that two new issues will rise in value. The Olympics stamps of 1972 should go up, especially the 6-cent and the 15-cent values, since these are rates not commonly used in great numbers. The 8-cent denomination will fall far behind the others, in my estimation.

The other issue that will rise is the National Parks Centennial in the 2-cent denomination, for reasons explained in another part of this book—the combined fact that it is *se-tenant* and composite, and of a denomination used as a "filler" rate rather than a standard postage rate. That it is our first composite also will help the rise.

The 6-cent denomination, the 11-cent air mail, and the 15-cent denomination should also enjoy a comfortable rise in value. The 11-cent air mail should because it is a good-looking stamp, a popular rate for domestic postage, and it took hold immediately upon release, everyone buying it as fast as they could until post office stocks were quickly exhausted. The fact is, the entire issue of these stamps was so popular that stocks were quickly diminished in post offices, and people were turned away from the windows. The rush was on!

My own experience with the 11-cent air mail stamp of the parks will illustrate the idea of how a stamp will take hold, and how it will create such a demand that the value will increase. When the stamps were issued I went to my local post office just a few days later to get a sheet. Sold out. Not only that, I was told that they had sold out the first day it was available. There are, within a radius of about fifteen miles from where I live, some fourteen or fifteen local post offices. I went the rounds and found only two single stamps in one post office!

By now I was determined to find some of these elusive items, so I drove many miles to the nearest large city where, in the main post office, I finally was able to get the stamp. Then, just because I had had such difficulty in getting stock, I purchased two sheets instead of my usual one. The clerk who waited on me sold them to me with the remark that he had only a very few sheets left in stock and would not be getting any more.

There is no doubt that this stamp is still available in Washington, D.C., at the philatelic sales office, but the point is, the immediate or nearly immediate sellout in local post offices cannot but help boost the rise in price of the stamp. It creates a frantic attempt to buy it which would otherwise not be present. In my own case, I spent the better part of two days locating them. Certainly I am not alone in this. There must be tens of thousands of collectors who had the same problem and who went around their local countryside hunting for a post office which still had some in stock. I will bet that when most of these collectors finally did find some, they bought more than they normally would have purchased if they had been able to walk into their local office and get them without a problem.

Still, with my purchase of two sheets of this stamp and the subsequent purchase of two sheets each of all the other denominations in the set—this to make my stock complete with two sets of the complete issue—I am not investing. An investment purchase would be twenty-five, fifty, or one hundred sheets of any given stamp. Then investors who are going to cater to the block collectors for high-priced sales returns would purchase the same number of sheets in all the possible positions of the plate number, necessitating four times the number of sheets they would salt away in their safes. Of course, such purchases merely help boost the eventual price—until the stock is dumped into a ready market. When this happens, the price is bound to fall. Sometimes it falls so far in the case of foreign stamps that the investor suffers a loss on his purchase price.

As I stated earlier, this can rarely happen in United States postage unless—and this is the only time it would happen—an investor has several hundred sheets of stamps he must unload, with the plate number blocks removed, and offers them to a dealer. That dealer will buy the postage at 5 per cent or 10 per cent off face value to take them off the investor's hands.

The dealer will sink his money in the stock, making an immediate 5 per cent or 10 per cent profit, since the stamps are still worth their face value, in hope that the single stamps will go up. He hasn't much danger of losing even if it doesn't go up. He just has his money tied up. Many dealers in approvals buy stamps in this fashion—at a small discount off face, then use the stamps as postage in sending out their approval selections. This way they immediately get their small profit in the use at face value, the person receiving the approvals is delighted to find a commemorative stamp on the envelope, happily adding it free to his collecting, and the dealer has increased his future business. Since a large approval company sends out tens of thousands of selections per year, they use an enormous number of postage stamps.

Investment buying of postage stamps is a good hobby and a good way to make a buck if you are already rich. It is a good way to lose your shirt if you are not rich enough to play with a lot of money, or if you don't know all the ins and outs of philately.

Chapter Thirteen

People on Stamps

While most foreign countries put portraits of famous persons on their stamps in commemoration of some event or other, the United States uses pictures of actual persons on its stamp only after that person is dead.

In almost any school course, it will help if you know something about famous people connected with that subject. When projects are made for school presentation, a stamp or stamps showing the person about whom the paper is written would make a good display item. Knowing who has been shown on stamps can be useful in many different ways, and for this reason a list of famous people depicted on stamps of the United States is given

Most stamps of the Confederate states were crudely printed on poor-quality paper. Some are quite valuable now.

here, listed alphabetically by name, and by Scott Catalog number.

In all instances I have listed the catalogue number for the first stamp on which the portrait of the person appeared. Several persons appear on more than one stamp—Benjamin Franklin and George Washington in particular since both have been used as the design for dozens of stamps, both postage and revenue. But in most instances the person appears only one time.

With the exception of the list of Secretaries of the Treasury, I have not listed revenue stamps, nor have I listed stamps for the Confederate States of America.

Albert Gallatin—1279

James A. Garfield—205

Guiseppi Garibaldi—1168

Walter F. George—1170

Mahatma Ghandi—1174

Robert H. Goddard—C 69

George W. Goethals—856

Samuel Gompers—988

Alexander D. Goode—956

Ulysess S. Grant—223

Horace Greely—1177

Nathaniel Greene—785

Lieutenant Thomas Grosvenor—1361

Johann Gutenberg—1014

Nathan Hale—551

Alexander Hamilton—143

Dag Hammarskjold—1203

Wm. C. Handy—1372

Warren G. Harding—553

Joel Chandler Harris—980

Benjamin Harrison—308

William Henry Harrison—814

Rutherford B. Hayes—563

Patrick Henry—1052

Victor Herbert—881

Oliver Wendell Holmes—1288

Herbert Hoover—1269

Mark Hopkins—870

Sam Houston—776

Elias Howe—892

Charles E. Hughes—1195

Cordell Hull—1235

Washington Irving—859

Andrew Jackson—73

Thomas J. ("Stonewall") Jackson—788

John Jay—1046

Thomas Jefferson—12

Andrew Johnson—822

Louis Jolliet—1356

"Casey" Jones—993

John Paul Jones—790

Chief Joseph—1364

Kamehameha Ist—799

John F. Kennedy—1246

Francis Scott Key—962

Tadeusz Kosciuszko—734

Lajos Kossuth—1117

Marquis de Lafayette—1010

Fiorello La Guardia—not yet numbered

Sidney Lanier—1446

Jason Lee—964

Robert E. Lee—788

Meriwether Lewis—1063

Abraham Lincoln—77

Robert R. Livingston—323

Dr. Crawford W. Long—875

Henry W. Longfellow—864

Juliette Gordon Low—974

James Russell Lowell—866

Douglas A. MacArthur—1424

Thomas MacDonough—791

Edward A. MacDowell—882

James Madison—262

Winifred Scott—142

John Sevier—941

William H. Seward—370

Chief Shadoo—683

William Shakespeare—1250

Philip H. Sheridan—787

William T. Sherman—225

Alfred E. Smith—937

John Smith—328

John Philip Sousa—880

Edwin M. Stanton—138

Elizabeth Stanton—959

Baron Von Steuben—689

Adlai Stevenson—1275

Harlan F. Stone—965

Lucy Stone—1293

Gilbert C. Stuart—884

Peter Stuyvesant—971

John Sullivan—657

Sun Yat Sen—906

Robert A. Taft—1161

William Howard Taft—685

Zachary Taylor—179

Henry David Thoreau—1327

John Tyler—815

Martin Van Buren—813

Booker T. Washington—873

George Washington—2

John P. Washington—956

Martha Washington—306

Anthony Wayne—680

Daniel Webster—226

Noah Webster—1121

Joseph West—683

James A. Whistler—885

William A. White—960

Walt Whitman—867

Eli Whitney—889

John Greenleaf Whittier—865

Harvey Wiley—1080

Roger Williams—777

Francis E. Williard—872

Woodrow Wilson—623

Frank Lloyd Wright—1280

Orville Wright—C 45

Wilbur Wright—C 45

In addition to the list of famous people given above, the following Secretaries of the Treasury of the United States appear on stamps of the Department of Internal Revenue:

G. M. Bibb

G. W. Campbell

Salmon P. Chase

Howell Cobb

Thomas Corwin

William H. Crawford

Alexander Dallas

Samuel Dexter

J. A. Dix

William J. Duane

Thomas Ewing

C. J. Folger

Walter Forward   Richard Rush
L. J. Gage   J. C. Spencer
Albert Gallatin   Roger B. Taney
W. Q. Gresham   P. F. Thomas
James Guthrie   R. J. Walker
Alexander Hamilton   William Windom
S. D. Ingham   Oliver Wolcott, Jr.
Louis McLane   Levi Woodbury
William M. Meredith

The face values of these tax stamps run from 1 cent to $10,000, and all of them are inscribed *Documentary*. Since these men appear on so many documentary stamps, I have omitted the catalogue numbers.

Throughout the world, many famous people can be found on stamps of some country. Famous people of the world forms one of the largest topical selections in stamp collecting and affords an excellent education in world affairs, politics, science, and the arts.

Chapter Fourteen

Luminescence on Stamps

In 1962 the United States received shipments of paper containing a luminescent dye which caused the paper, when exposed to "black light" (ultraviolet light) to glow with an intense whitish-violet radiance. This paper was called Brite, or Hi-brite, and it was used for printing stamps, the luminescent properties being then unknown. These were the first luminescent stamps issued, and they were, of course, unintentionally produced.

The dye used in making the paper is water soluble, and used stamps, soaked off the paper, lose the quality of luminescence. Therefore, it is important to test the stamps before soaking them, and any printed on Hi-brite paper should be left on the entire envelope or cut off with some of the envelope surrounding the stamp, leaving the stamp tied to this piece of paper.

In the year 1963 the government began experiments in "tagging" stamps with phosphorescent or luminescent inks for purposes of sorting in high-speed automatic machines. These experiments were carried out in the Dayton, Ohio, post office, and were successful. Nearly all stamps now issued by the postal service are tagged in one way or another. The ink used for definitive postage stamps phosphoresces a bright yellow-green, and that used for air mail postage phosphoresces brilliant orange-red to red-orange. The machines used in sorting mail have color-sensitive cells that can differentiate between these colors, and they can with amazing speed and accuracy sort the air mail pieces from the regular mail, sending them to separate bins, for further sorting and distribution.

Since, in the early days of tagging, some stamp sheets went through without the tagging ink being applied, these were immediately sought after as "errors" by stamp collectors, with a resulting jump in value. As is the usual case with any such incidence of popularity, unscrupulous persons also immediately began to find ways of creating such "errors" in counterfeit.

It was discovered that a tagged stamp, subjected to the fumes of certain acids, lost the luminescent properties, and these treated stamps found their way into the stamp market in large quantities. So large, in fact, that reputable stamp dealers have discontinued considering untagged varieties of normally tagged stamps as errors, and the price of such copies has stopped rising.

Fortunately or unfortunately, however you may look at it, these acid treated stamps reveal themselves in time. After several months or a few years, the stamps become very brittle and/or discolored. The inks may bleach. The stamp itself cannot be touched or it will fall apart in fragments. This is the fortunate part—detection of a counterfeit. The unfortunate part being that the stamp, for which you may have paid a premium price, is lost forever, and you have become wiser but sadder.

Hi-brite paper is another thing. This cannot as yet be counterfeited, or rather, ordinary paper cannot be made Hi-brite. So those stamps still have value above normal paper.

Tagging stamps is done in several different ways or types. First, the ink is applied with either rolls, mats, or plates, flat or curved. Type I tagging is done with a mat or a set of mats. In the full sheet as it comes from the presses, four mats are used to apply the luminescent ink.

Type II tagging is done with a roll, the sheets of stamps being passed under the roll carrying the ink.

Type III tagging is done with a curved plate that

is rocked across the sheets of stamps to apply the ink.

Type OP tagging is used on multicolored stamps after they have been printed on the Giori press.

Type B tagging is a bar applied to the printed area of the stamp and not over the entire sheet of stamps. This type of tagging does not extend, or should not extend, beyond the printed limits of the design.

Type GB tagging is a rectangle of luminescent ink applied to the paper at one side of the stamp on postal stationery; postal cards, stamped envelopes, etc. Here the ink does not fall on the printed stamp area, but on the stationery beside the stamp, and the specimen, if used, should be cut with enough of the paper remaining to carry the tag.

Type AC tagging is used also on postal stationery and has the luminescent ink mixed with the printing ink. These stamps—an example being the Paul Revere postal card—carry no visible (or invisible) bar of luminescence, but the design of the stamp itself glows under the black light.

Some of the stamps known to have been printed on Hi-brite paper are listed here so you can identify any that may turn up in your collection. They are listed by both the Scott Catalog number and, in parentheses, the Minkus Catalog number.

1031 (570) 1¢ green
1035 (573) 3¢ deep violet

1036 (574) 4¢ red-violet
1040 (577) 7¢ rose-carmine
1044 (580) 10¢ rose lake
1046 (592) 15¢ rose lake
1047 (581) 20¢ ultramarine
1048 (593) 25¢ green
1058 (590) 4¢ red-violet (coil)
1209 (607) 1¢ green
1213 (604) 5¢ dark blue-gray
1229 (605) 5¢ dark blue-gray (coil)
1244 (CM529) 5¢ blue-green
C 64 (A64) 8¢ carmine (air mail)
C 65 (A65) 8¢ carmine (air mail coil)

There may be others, but these are the only ones I have been able to turn up. It would be a good policy to check all stamps from now on to see if any new specimens do show up on Hi-brite paper, and if so, put them aside until it is determined whether or not they are to be held at a premium.

About 1970 the Bureau of Printing and Engraving decided that the paper used for printing stamps could have a brightening content (fluorescent dye) and still be permitted. This paper would fall into the category of Brite, but not the flaming Hi-brite. Stamps printed on such paper are not held at premium prices, but if any slipped through on Hi-brite, they would be considered errors.

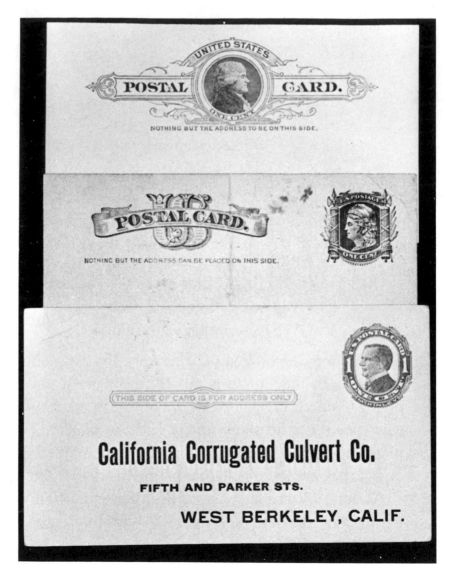

A group of early postal cards.

Chapter Fifteen

Post Cards, Envelopes, and First Day Covers

The cards issued by the government with stamps already printed on them are really not post cards, but postal cards. The distinction being that post cards are without stamps, and are usually scenic cards printed to advertise some place or event and sold as tourist items. While collecting post cards is a big hobby, too, we are concerned in this book only with postal cards and stamped envelopes as sold at post offices throughout the United States and possessions.

Postal cards are made in two ways—as a regular card, having a stamp printed in the upper right-hand corner, and with or without the admonition that the stamped side of the card is for the address only—and as a message-reply card. In the latter case the card is double, folded on a rouletted line so the two parts can be easily separated. Each card has a stamp printed on it, and one card is for your message; the other card is for the recipient's reply to you, the postage already having been paid by you when you purchased the reply card. Such message-reply cards should be preserved intact. They have more value than if the two parts are separated.

Postal cards are now made in both regular mail and air mail types. Usually, but not always, the air mail types have a red-and-blue border of diagonal bars to attract attention to the fact that it is being sent via air. With the modern high-speed sorting machines operating on tagged stamps instead of visual determination, the border is not any longer necessary. However, it is still used.

Postal cards and envelopes may be tagged with the GB type of tagging in which the glow-bar of luminescent ink is placed on the card or envelope beside the impression of the stamp, but not touching it. Or they may be tagged by the AC type of tagging in which the luminescent dye is mixed with the printing ink, causing the entire design of the stamp to glow under the detecting cell in the sorting machine.

The first postal cards were issued in the year 1873, and they have been continuously issued since that time. Up until 1920 the designs were changed every two to five years. The 1920 designs ran until 1926, then no new issue was printed until 1951.

Whereas the stamps on postal cards were for many years just portraits of the various Presidents, in recent times we have been dressing up the stamps and now have begun to use decorative designs for the impressions. Postal cards are collected in the entire condition. That is to say, the stamps are not cut from the card to be placed in the collection.

Beginning in 1910, postal cards have been printed by the Government Printing Office. In 1886 the first rotary presses were put into use with the printing of the postal card issued in that year. All postal cards and all stamped envelopes are printed only on watermarked stock, as opposed to regular postage stamps which are on unwatermarked paper.

Envelopes were first printed in 1953 by private printing companies who submitted bids to the government for the contract to produce the envelopes. Each four years a new bidding is held, and as a result the companies printing envelopes change from time to time.

Private printing also accounts for different shades in the color of the paper and in different weights of the paper. Watermarks usually are changed at each bidding, but it is permitted to use the remaining stock of paper before starting the new stock. This makes varieties in color, weight, and watermark in envelopes.

Stamped envelopes are collected as entire or cut squares. If the stamp is cut from the envelope, a margin of at least one-fourth inch should be left all around the design. If the stamp is cut to outline, it has a far lesser value than a cut square. Only in certain cases is a cut-to-shape envelope stamp of any real value. While an entire envelope has a somewhat greater value than the cut square, the collecting of envelope stamps in this fashion requires the use of special envelope or cover albums. They are most difficult to mount in a regular album and will stretch the pockets of a stock book to the point where they will no longer contain any stamps placed in them.

Stamped envelopes are made in several sizes—the same stamp appearing on each. Usually, there is no difference in value between the sizes. Exceptions to this rule are, of course, plentiful.

While the United States does not surcharge its postage stamps, it does revalue both postal cards and envelopes. Some of this revaluing was done at the post office by affixing a stamp of the current issue to the card before sale, to make up the deficit in face value. Others were printed with a revaluing impression, whether stating the amount of revaluation or simply that the stamp had been revalued. In this case, although the stamp read one value, it was charged for at the new postal rate for that type of mail. Often surcharges were used on envelopes,

Stamped envelopes. When fine cancellations are available it is good to leave enough of the envelope to contain the entire cancellation.

with a series of bars or lines obliterating the old value, with the new value appearing as a large numeral or word over the face of the stamp impression.

First day covers are a method of collecting stamps on envelopes that have been mailed with a cancellation showing clearly that the envelope was mailed on the day the stamp was first issued from the place of issue commemorating that stamp.

Each stamp printed for postal service is first placed on sale in the post office of whatever city is pertinent to the issue. If it commemorates a famous person, as an example, the first day of issue would more than likely be the city in which that person was born. If the stamp is in commemoration of some historical or national event or landmark, the first day issue location would be the city nearest

Some commemorative stamped envelopes. The lower group has been revalued by the government to match the going postage rate.

the place where the event occurred or the landmark was located.

While the new issue of stamps is sent to post offices all over the country, the postmasters are instructed to withhold the sale of them until the day after the day of issue. This means that if the first day sale is on the first of the month, local post offices in other than the first day city cannot sell the stamps until the second of that month.

First day covers have become a big thing in stamp collecting, and several companies are now engaged in printing very elaborate envelopes for sale as first day covers. Perhaps the leading company in this is White Ace, who put out beautifully engraved envelopes for each stamp to be issued. Naturally, these envelopes are available some time before the stamp is to be issued, since they must be purchased by the individual collectors, addressed, and sent to the postmaster at the post office in the first-day-of-issue city, in time for the stamps to be affixed there and the envelope and stamp canceled

A first day cover honoring the stamp issued for General Patton.

with the special canceling die made for the purpose.

The procedure is to address as many envelopes as you wish to yourself, or your friends, and send them, together with a money order for the amount of postage required, to the first-day-issue postmaster in the proper location. He will then affix a stamp or stamps to each envelope, canceling them with the special die, and mail them back to you. There is no fee attached other than the cost of the stamps involved.

Every post office has a bulletin board on which, long in advance of the date of issue, new stamps are advertised, together with the date of issue and the first-day-issue post office. You merely have to keep reading these bulletins to keep abreast of new stamps.

The Superintendent of Documents, Government Printing Office, Washington, D.C. 20402 sells subscriptions at $6.00 per year to the "Postal Bulletin." This is issued weekly, and contains information on current orders for stamp printings, as well as philatelic information on our stamps, and all other information about the postal service of the United States. For serious collectors and investors, this is a good buy. The catalogue number for ordering a subscription is: P-1.3. You may subscribe to this bulletin for one, two, or three years, but no longer than three years at a time.

Chapter Sixteen

Gimmick Stamps

In the last few years several countries have issued gimmick stamps. These are stamps printed on material other than paper, made in odd and irregular shapes, with a different kind of adhesive than the regular gum used on ordinary stamps.

Perhaps it is not fair to call these stamps "gimmicks," although, in the minds of most serious collectors and dealers, that is what they are. Make no mistake about their value. When one set of stamps issued by the island of Tonga was first out, it went begging for buyers. The prices remained small for years, until very recently, when suddenly collectors wishing to add them to their collections were unpleasantly surprised to find the value of the stamps going up rapidly, and they are continuing to rise!

Tonga and Sierra Leone issue stamps printed on foil, with a self-adhesive gum covered by a peelable paper back. These stamps were first in the design of coins minted by the two countries and were issued to commemorate the minting of the money.

Tonga then, it seems, went all out in gimmick stamps and has issued some rather odd specimens, to say the least. One stamp, also on foil, is in the shape of the island itself. The country has also is-

"Hardware" and "gimmick" stamps from Tonga. These are now increasing in values.

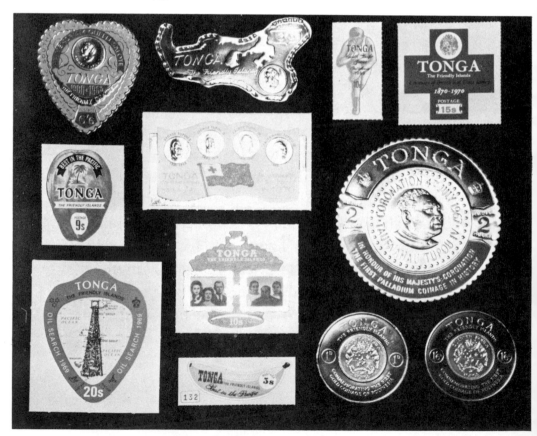

sued many self-adhesive stamps in very bizarre shapes, printed on paper, and backed with a peelable paper bearing various slogans.

Sierra Leone has issued such adhesive stamps, and the backing paper on these carry advertisements for various firms, among them a Mercedes-Benz automobile agency! Doubtless the country realizes a revenue from this advertisement, augmenting that received from the sale of the stamps.

Tonga has issued stamps in the shape and color of coconuts, bananas, a foot racer, the Red Cross, an open book, and many others. These are all peelable and self-adhesive, and when once affixed to an envelope are practically impossible to remove. Canceled stamps of this type should be collected on full cover or, at least, cut square as though they were printed on the envelope.

Bhutan and other countries have issued stamps in so-called "3-D" printing. These are made the same way as the very beautiful post cards from Japan, on which the pictures look as though they were in three dimensions. The stamps are issued by the same printing process and are indeed beautiful. Some of them are now very costly, especially the souvenir sheets of the space issues.

An amusing incident connected with these kinds of stamps happened while writing this book. Not being a collector of gimmick stamps myself, I was forced to look for specimens to photograph for il-

A photograph cannot show the beautiful "3-D" effect of these stamps from Bhutan.

lustrations. I was unable to find any local collector who had them, so I went to a dealer and purchased a collection. When I got home I discovered to my amusement that the cash receipt was made out as "Hardware," instead of stamps—indicative of that particular dealer's opinion of the foil stamps. I noticed, however, that his opinion did not reduce the prices he charged me for them.

Chapter Seventeen

Precanceled Stamps

In an effort to save time in the post offices, where the clerks had to run mail through canceling machines, or cancel them by hand, the government authorized the precanceling of stamps.

These stamps were sold only to companies having large mailing lists and possessing or applying for a permit for bulk mail. The idea being that by affixing precanceled stamps to the bulk mail, then delivering it to the post office bundled up, the clerks could send the mail directly through the sorters without having to take the time to cancel the stamps.

Until very recently precanceled stamps were restricted to such sales. Now, however, individuals

Some precanceled stamps. Coils were also precanceled. Now an individual may purchase them in limited quantities.

A wavy line precanceled stamp, which may be used anywhere in the United States, and the regular stamp shown for comparison.

may purchase them in limited quantities, either from post offices in cities having precancels, or from the Philatelic•Bureau in Washington, D.C.

Naturally, precanceled stamps printed with the name of a city and state could only be used for mail from that city. This makes the number of pre-cancels reach an astronomical figure, since many values of stamps were precanceled for each major city in the country.

A second type of precanceling has been intro-duced that permits the use of the stamps from any post office in the United States. This is in the form of two or three bars printed on the stamp. The bars may be straight or wavy, and they usually do not impinge on the stamp design, but run to either side, as in the case of postal cards. The stamps this type of precanceling was applied to were the Christmas issue of toys of 1970, and the stamps were sold in sixty-nine cities in the country.

These were, by the way, one of the few stamps devalued by the government, since the precanceled variety was permitted for use only for a limited time—I believe until January 31 of the year follow-ing their issue. Of course, only half of the entire is-sue was precanceled; the remaining half being sold as regular stamps, which are still usable as postage if you happen to have any and want to mail letters with them.

Besides being applied to sheet stamps, precanceling was done on coil stamps also for bulk mailing.

Because of the way they were restricted, the collecting of mint precancels is a difficult thing, except for recent issues available now by individuals. A complete collection of mint precancels would have a considerable value today.

Chapter Eighteen

Other Philatelic Items

Besides postage stamps, postal cards, stamped envelopes, and other kinds of postal service items, collectors eagerly search for items connected with postal service that are not actually for postal duty. The exception to this statement are special delivery stamps, which are used as postage without the use of a regular postage stamp in conjunction.

The United States has issued two types of air post special delivery stamps, now obsolete. A registration stamp was first issued in 1855, and registration stamps continued to be in use until 1913. In 1955 a special stamp for certified mail was issued. It was intended for use when proof of mailing without indemnity value was required.

Certified mail stamps may not be used for any other kind of mail. They have now been discontinued.

The different governmental departments—the War Department, the State Department, the Department of Agriculture, etc.—used to issue stamps for their own use. These stamps were in use from 1873 to 1884. Little is known of their history. Some of them command enormous prices, especially in mint condition. They are called official stamps, and the catalogues list them as such.

Newspaper and periodical stamps were in use from 1899 to 1965 for the bulk shipment of such printed matter.

Postal note stamps were used from 1945 to 1951 to supplement the money-order service.

In 1912 the government issued a set of twelve

Postal note stamps were issued to augment money orders. Used for smaller amounts, they are no longer valid.

stamps intended for use only on parcel post mail. This is one of the nicest sets of stamps this country has ever issued, each stamp depicting an urban or rural scene or industry. At the same time, a set of five parcel postage-due stamps was issued, to cover parcels mailed with insufficient postage.

Regular postage-due stamps were first issued in the year 1879 and are still in use today. They are for the collection at the delivery end of postage due on mail sent without the correct amount affixed.

The year 1872 saw the first appearance of post office seals. At first these were intended to be placed over the flap of registered mail envelopes, sealing them so they could not be tampered with. In 1949 the words "opened through mistake by" were added

Official seals are still used. They are used only by postal employees.

to the designs of post office seals, and these were used to reseal letters that had been opened mistakenly for one reason or another. The seal was folded over the opened end of the envelope, holding

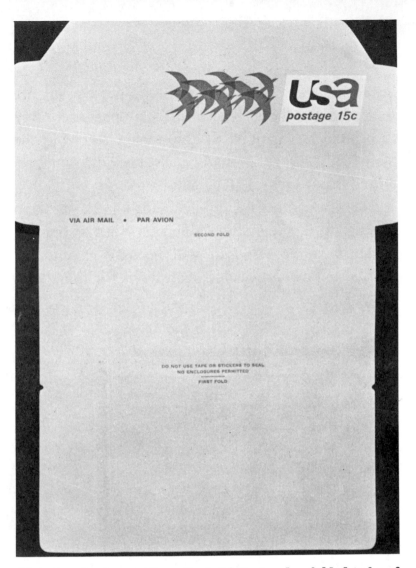

VIA AIR MAIL • PAR AVION

SECOND FOLD

DO NOT USE TAPE OR STICKERS TO SEAL
NO ENCLOSURES PERMITTED

FIRST FOLD

Air letter sheets must be collected intact and unfolded to be of philatelic value.

it together with its contents inside, and delivered to the addressee in that condition—signed by the postal clerk who opened the mail. The addressee had little to say about his mail having been opened.

Air letter sheets, cut to a shape that permits the sender to fold it into an envelope with the writing inside and the stamp on the proper corner, are sold at post offices. These are slit open according to printed instructions by the person receiving the mail. Unlike regular mail, enclosures are not permitted inside an air letter sheet.

There are other philatelic items—most of them obscure to the beginning collector—that as one becomes more experienced will become of interest. Specialized catalogues list such items for those who are interested.

A kind of souvenir card sold by the government to collectors.

Chapter Nineteen

Identification of Stamps

Every now and then a stamp will turn up with no identification as to what country issued it. That is, they *seem* to have no identification to a beginner who is not familiar with the different symbols used by certain countries. A short list is offered here of some of the more common identification markings. This list is by no means complete, but will help identify stamps that are liable to turn up in packets, sets, or in approval books.

A—*Columbia, overprint on air mail stamps.*

A & T—*Annam and Tonkin, overprint on French colonial stamps for use in Annam and Tonkin.*

A.B.—*Far Eastern Republic, overprinted on Russian stamps.*

A.C.C.P.—*Azerbaijan.*

A.E.F—*French Equatorial Africa*

ANDORRA—*Spanish Andorra*

ANDORRE—*French Andorra.*

A.O.—*German East Africa (Belgian occupation).*

A.O.F.—*French West Africa, overprint on French stamps.*

A.O.I—*Italian East Africa, overprint on Italian stamps.*

ARCHIPEL DES COMORES—*Comoro Islands.*

A.R.COLON—*Panama, occupation by Columbia.*

AUNUS—*Russia, overprint on Finnish stamps for Finnish occupation of Russia.*

AYTONOME—*Epirus.*

BANAT NACSKA—*Hungary.*

BAYERN—*Bavaria.*

B.C.A.—*British Central Africa, overprint on Rhodesian stamps.*

BELGIE—*Belgium.*

BELGIQUE—*Belgium.*

BENADIR—*Italian Somaliland.*

BOGACHES—*Yemen.*

BOGCHAH—*Yemen.*

BOGSHA—*Yemen.*

BOHMEN UND MAHREN—*Czechoslovakia.*

BOLLO DELLA POSTA NAPOLETANA—*Two Sicilies Italy.*

BOLLO POSTALE—*San Marino.*

BOSNIEN HERZEGOWINA—*Bosnia and Herzegovina.*
BUITER BEZIT—*Dutch East Indies.*

CAMBODGE—*Cambodia (Indo-China).*
C.C.C.P.—*Russia.*
CECHY A MORAVIA—*Czechoslovakia*
C. CH—*Cochin, overprint on French stamps.*
C.E.F.—*Cameroun, overprint on German stamps for British use in occupation of Cameroun.*
CEZKOSLOVENSKO—*Czechoslovakia.*
C.F.A.—*Réunion, overprint on French stamps for use in Réunion.*
C.G.H.S.—*Upper Silesia, overprint on German and Prussian stamps.*
CHALA—*Peru, overprint used by Chilean occupation forces.*
CHEMINS DE FER—*Belgium, overprint for use as parcel post stamps.*
C.I.H.S.—*Germany, overprint for use in Upper Silesia.*
CO. CI.—*Yugoslavia (Croatia) for use during Italian occupation.*
C.X.C.—*Yugoslavia (Croatia).*

DANSK VESTINDIEN—*Danish West Indies.*
DARDANELLES—*Russia, overprint for use in Turkey.*
DDR—*East Germany (German Democratic Republic).*
DESMIT RBL—*Latvia.*

DEUTSCHE BUNDEPOST—*West Germany.*

DEUTSCHES REICH—*Germany.*

DIWI RUBLI—*Latvia.*

D.P.B.—*Far Eastern Republic, overprint on Russian stamps.*

DRZAVA S.H.S.—*Croatia (Yugoslavia) for use in Bosnia and Herzegovina.*

E.A.F.—*Great Britain, overprint for use in Italian Somaliland.*

E.E.F.—*Palestine, for use during British occupation.*

EIRE—*Ireland.*

EUPEN—*Germany, overprint on Belgian stamps.*

GPE or G.P.E.—*Overprint on French stamps for use in Guadeloupe.*

G.W.—*Griqualand, overprint on Cape of Good Hope stamps.*

HEDJAZ & NEDJE—*Saudi Arabia.*

HEJAZ & NEJD—*Saudi Arabia.*

HELVETIA—*Switzerland.*

HERZOGTH-SCHLESWIG—*Holstein (Prussia).*

H RV—*Croatia.*

HRVATSKA—*Croatia.*

H.R.Z.C.L. POST F.R.M.—*Holstein.*

ISLAND—*Iceland.*

K.60 K.—*Armenia, overprint on Russian stamps.*

KOZTARSASAG—*Hungary (early stamps).*

K.U.K. FELDPOST—*Austria.*

LATTAQUIE—*Latakia, overprint on Syrian stamps.*

LATVIJA or LATWIJA—*Latvia.*

L'ININI—*Inini, overprint on French Guiana stamps* for use in Inini.

LJUBLJANSKA—*Yugoslavia (Croatia).*

L.P. LATVIA—*Overprint on Russian stamps for use in Latvia.*

L.T.S.R.—*Lithuania.*

MAGYAR—*Hungary.*

MAGYAR KIR POSTA—*Hungary.*

MAGYAR TANACS KOZTARSASAG—*Hungarian Soviet Republic.*

MALMEDY—*Belgium.*

M.Q.E.—*Martinique, overprint on French colonial stamps for use in Martinique.*

M.V.i.R.—*Romania, overprint on German stamps.*

N.D. HRVATSKA—*Croatia.*

N.D. RATNI DOPRINOS—*Croatia.*

NORGE—*Norway.*

N.S.B.—*Nossi-Bé.*

POCZTA—*Poland.*

POCZTA-LITWA SRODKOWA—*Central Lithuania.*

POCZTA POLSKA—*Poland.*

POHJOIS INKERI—*North Ingermanland.*

QARKU—*Albania.*

R.O.—*Eastern Rumelia, overprint on British stamps.*
RSM—*San Marino.*

SOUDAN FAIS—*French Sudan.*
S.P.M.—*St. Pierre and Miquelon, overprint on French colonial stamps.*
SRODKOWA LITWA—*Central Lithuania.*
SUOMI—*Finland.*

TICAL—*Siam (Thailand).*
TIRANE KALLNUER—*Albania.*
TOGA—*Tonga (early stamps).*

VAN DIEMEN'S LAND—*Tasmania (early stamps).*
VRIJ—*Orange River Colony.*

WENDEN—*Russia.*
WENDENSCHEN—*Russia.*

Glossary

———

There are many terms used in philately that are not commonly used in any other place in our language, and it is conceivable that some of them are completely foreign to a beginner. A list of some terms is appended here for your convenience.

Bisects—This term means a stamp that has been cut to be used for a lesser postage value than its face. For example, a 10-cent stamp may be cut in half and used as a 5-cent stamp. This was permitted long ago, but it is no longer allowed. There are three types of bisects—horizontal, vertical, and diagonal. Bisecting was done in emergencies when no stamps of the lower denomination were available.

Booklet Pane—Stamps are issued in booklets containing a certain amount of stamps of one or more denominations, for convenience in carrying in ladies' handbags, for example, or in men's wallets. A booklet pane is the entire sheet of stamps that is contained in such a booklet. In this country, this

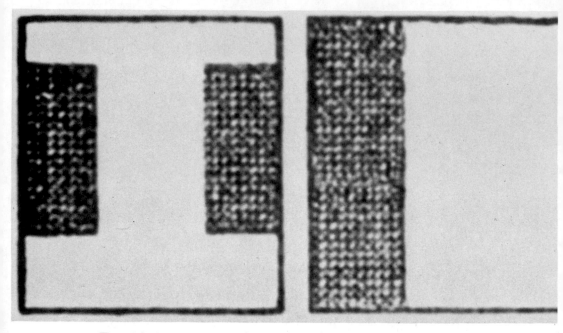

Two kinds of grills applied to United States stamps. When the stamp is canceled, the ink runs through the paper fibers, prohibiting removal.

sheet usually consists of eight stamps although a pane may contain only four, five, six, or seven stamps, the other spaces taken up by labels.

Canceled—This term means that the stamp was used for postage.

Canceled-to-order—Many countries cancel stamps for sale to collectors without the stamps ever having seen postal duty. They are mint stamps with a lightly applied cancellation.

Double Impression—A printing plate for stamps is made by transferring each design to a large plate by means of a hardened roller bearing one impression. Sometimes this roller skips when transferring the design, resulting in a double impression on the finished plate. Stamps printed from such a plate are classed among errors. Double impressions have not occurred for many years in the printing of United States postage.

Error—An error is any stamp that differs from the normal stamp by reason of some mistake in printing, the use of the wrong paper, an incorrect color, or for any other reason. Usually errors are very costly, since they are far less in quantity than the normal stamp, and the demand far exceeds the supply.

A cross-gutter block.

First Day Cover—This is purely a philatelic term applied to a complete envelope bearing a stamp and with or without a cachet (picture) depicting a scene for which the stamp was issued in commemoration. It also bears a clear cancellation dated on the day the stamp was first placed on sale.

Giori Press—A comparatively new press, imported from Italy, on which it is possible to print multicolored stamps at high speed. Most of the stamps of the United States are now printed on the Giori press. We have also other new types of presses, the multicolored Huck press, the Cottrell press, and others, in addition to the older rotary presses and the flat-bed presses. The 7-cent stamp bearing a likeness of Benjamin Franklin released on October 20, 1972, was printed on the Cottrell press.

Grill—In past years, stamps were grilled in order to make it impossible to remove the cancellations and reuse the stamp. A grill is a block of impressions pressed into the paper to the point of actually breaking the surface of the paper. When the stamp is canceled, the canceling ink penetrates the broken paper, coloring the paper clear through. Grills were placed on stamps either as blocks of impressions in the centers of each individual stamp in the sheet, a line of grilling running down the side of each row of stamps, or two parallel lines running down both sides of each row of stamps. Grilling is no longer used on United States stamps.

A provisional stamp. This happens also to be a first day cover, making it of double interest.

Gutter—When stamps are printed in full sheets, there are four panes to a sheet with a wide margin between the sheets. This margin is called a gutter. In certain stamps gutter pairs or gutter blocks are available—notably in the "Farley's Follies" several stamps reissued by the then postmaster, James Farley, to satisfy the clamorings of the philatelists who objected to the practice of presenting full sheets of stamps to persons by the Post Office Department. A gutter pair is two stamps separated by the wide gutter. A gutter block is four stamps, one at each corner of the wide gutter. When a sheet is cut into the four individual panes, the gutter is sliced through the middle, becoming the margin of the pane bearing the plate number and inscriptions.

Imperforate—This term simply means that the stamps in the sheet are as printed, without perforations running between each individual stamp. Such stamps must be cut from the sheet with scissors, rather than being separated by tearing apart as in regular perforate stamps.

Line Pair—In making coil stamps, every twenty-five stamps or so a line is printed between two stamps. Since this line appears only infrequently in coils, it brings a premium in price.

Luminescence—In 1963 the Post Office Department began experiments with stamps "tagged" with luminescent ink. This was to facilitate handling of mail, since high-speed machinery could sort and cancel mail so marked, picking out the afterglow of phosphorescent ink with the aid of electric-eye detectors. Two kinds of inks are used; orange-red-glowing for air mail, and yellow-green-glowing for regular mail. Now most if not all of the stamps issued are tagged with the luminescent ink, either as an overprint or incorporated in the ink used to print the stamps.

Mint—This term applies to a stamp that is fresh and new as it came from the presses. If the stamp is not in perfect condition, then the things wrong with it are listed along with the term mint.

Overprint—Anything printed on the face of a stamp that is not solely a change of face value. This includes a provisional overprint, overprinting to make a stamp of regular postal issue usable for revenue service, to make a stamp used only on official service, etc.

Paper—Many kinds of paper have been used for the printing of postage stamps, and the names of these papers may be unfamiliar to the reader. I list a few of them here, with descriptions for recognition:

A) *Double paper*—This was a patented paper made many years ago consisting of two layers. The top layer, on which the stamp was printed, would destruct if, for example, any attempt was made to remove a cancellation in order to reuse the stamp. The term double paper also applies to stamps printed on the joints of paper rolls. When coil stamps and rotary press stamps are made, the rolls of paper are pasted together at the end when going through the press in order to keep the paper continuous. This pasted joint is double, and the stamps printed over the joint are said to be printed on paste-up or double paper. They have some increased value over the regular issue.

B) *Granite*—Granite paper is the same as silk paper with the addition of a light gray dye added to the pulp. Our stamp commemorating Search for Peace, issued in 1967 was printed on granite paper.

C) *Laid*—This term applies to the way the paper is made. Laid paper is made by depositing the pulp on a screen belt having a very fine even mesh.

D) *Pelure*—Pelure is a semi-transparent paper, very thin, and usually stiff and hard.

E) *Silk*—This term applies to paper containing fine silk threads in the pulp from which it is made. United States paper money is also printed on silk paper.

F) *Wove*—Another term applying to the making of paper. Here the screen belt has parallel bars in the mesh, resulting in a design of parallel lines being impressed in the finished paper.

Plate Block—A block of stamps left attached to the margin strip bearing the plate number from which the stamps were printed. In rotary-press stamps this is a block of four; in flat-press stamps, a block of six; in Giori-press stamps having a number of plate numbers—one for each color—the block may number up to twenty stamps.

Position Blocks—This term applies to plate-number blocks of stamps in sets showing the plate numbers in all the positions made in the printing. The usual number of positions is four, upper right and left, and lower right and left.

Precancel—The United States Government authorizes the overprinting of certain stamps with a name of a city or town, precanceling the stamp before it has served its postal function. These stamps are then sold to companies having precanceling permits, who use them as postage, generally on parcel post. This was instigated to save time in the post offices, where such mail must be canceled by hand, rather than by machine. Precanceled stamps are not usually sold to individuals at post offices.

Provisional—When a new country is formed, which seems to be very often these days, some provision must be made to handle the mail while stamps are being designed and printed. Usually the stamps already in use in that country are overprinted with some identification to mark them as being used in the new country. Such is the case with Bangladesh. Bangladesh was formerly East Pakistan, and when they gained their independence and renamed their country, they used the stamps of East Pakistan with an overprint declaring the name of the new country. These are provisional stamps, and usually provisionals are very costly, since they are used only in an emergency period, being replaced by stamps definitive to the country at the earliest opportunity.

Roulette—A method of perforating stamps without punching a row of holes through the paper. Rouletting is a series of straight-line cuts instead of holes,

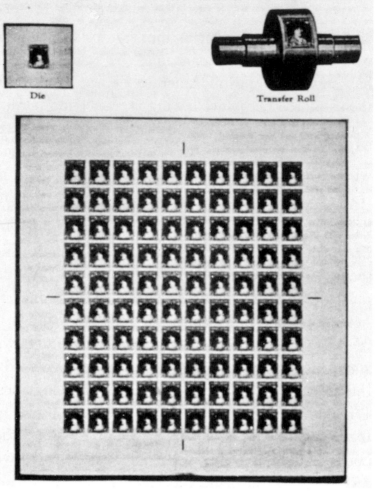

A printing plate, the die, and the transfer roll used to make the plate. (Photo from Scott's Standard Postage Stamp Catalog. Courtesy Scott Publishing Company.)

and the stamps are separated along these lines, leaving rough edges on the stamp.

Se-tenant—A French term used to describe stamps

printed adjacent to each other but with different designs, different values, or different colors.

Surcharge—A surcharge is a change of denomination printed on the face of a stamp. This can be because of a change of postage rate to a denomination for which there are no stamps available. In that instance, supplies of existing stamps of any denomination may have a new value printed on their face and then would be used to fulfill the new rate. In a sense, these are provisional stamps.

Tête-bêche—This is a French term, used in philately to describe two stamps that are attached to each other but carry the picture on one of them upside down in relation to the other.

Thinned—In handling stamps, often a hinge will be pulled off in the wrong way, resulting in the paper of the stamp being separated and part pulled away. This leaves a thin spot and, incidently, either completely ruins the stamp, or at the very best drops its value to next to nothing. Often thinning results from the stamp becoming stuck to another stamp or to an album page. The result is the same.

Tied On—A stamp is said to be tied to a cover when the cancellation covers both a part of the stamp and part of the cover.

Transfer—The method used in making a plate for

printing stamps. A die is cut and hardened. Then an impression is made on a roller of soft steel. This is the transfer roll, and it is hardened after taking the impression of the original die. The transfer roll is then rocked on the printing plate in the positions required to fill the plate with impressions for the full sheet of stamps. In this manner, identical impressions are made that otherwise would be most difficult to achieve.

Watermarked—This term is more fully described in the chapter devoted to watermarks. It pertains to a design made into the paper upon which stamps are printed.

INDEX

(

PAUL VILLIARD, the author of *Collecting Stamps,* was born in Spokane, Washington, and now lives in Saugerties, New York. Although he started out as a mechanical engineer, he soon found that his real talent lay in writing and photography.

He has traveled for many years in the Pacific Islands, South America, and throughout the United States. From these years of traveling, observing, and photographing, came much of the material for many of his books.

A stamp collector himself, Mr. Villiard's other books include *Wild Mammals as Pets, Reptiles as Pets, Insects as Pets,* and *Exotic Fish as Pets.* His beautiful photography and fine writing have appeared in *Natural History, Audubon Magazine, Popular Home Craft, Home Crafts and Hobbies, Reader's Digest,* and *Nature and Science* magazine, among others.